HEALING YOUR POISONED FAMILY TREE

Freedom from Generational Curses

J. E Charles

Copyright and Permissions
Healing Your Poisoned Family Tree
Revoking Evil Ancestral Vows
© 2021 J. E Charles

A publication of Dunamis Christian Center | Upper Room Fire Prayer Ministry
P.O Box 12352 Pleasanton CA 94588
Printed in the United States of America

All rights reserved. No part of this publication may be reproduced, stored in a retrieval system or be transmitted in any form or by any means, mechanical, electronic, photocopying or otherwise without prior written consent of the publisher.

Unless otherwise noted, all Scripture quotations are taken from the King James Version.

Scripture quotations marked (NIV) are taken from the Holy Bible, New International Version®, NIV®. Copyright © 1973, 1978, 1984, 2011 by Biblica, Inc.™ Used by permission of Zondervan. All rights reserved worldwide. www.zondervan.com The "NIV" and "New International Version" are trademarks registered in the United States Patent and Trademark Office by Biblica, Inc.™

Scripture quotations marked NLT are taken from the *Holy Bible*, New Living Translation, copyright 1996, 2004, 2007, 2015 by Tyndale House Foundation. Used by permission of Tyndale House Publishers, Inc., Carol Stream, Illinois 60188. All rights reserved.

Scripture quotations marked MSG are taken from THE MESSAGE, copyright © 1993, 2002, 2018 by Eugene H. Peterson. Used by permission of NavPress. All rights reserved. Represented by Tyndale House Publishers, a Division of Tyndale House Ministries.

Products are available at special quantity discounts for bulk purchase for sales promotion, premiums, fund-raising, and educational needs.

For details contact us at P. O. Box 12352, Pleasanton, CA 94588 or www.dunamisbookstore.com. Email: sales@upperroomfireprayer.org or Call 408 508 4304

Library of Congress Cataloging in-Publication Data: An application to register this book for cataloging has been submitted to the Library of Congress.

International Standard Book Number:
ISBN: 978-1-7362288-6-9
Pastor J. E Charles
Dunamis Publishing House
P.O. Box 340507, Jamaica, NY 11234 Email: info@upperroomfireprayer.org
Web: dunamisbookstore.com
Phone: +1 408.508.4304

DISCLAIMER

This book contains general information about spiritual deliverance. The information is not intended as medical advice and is not an alternative to medical advice from your doctor or other healthcare provider. By using the information contained in this book, the user assumes full responsibility for his or her actions and agrees that Pastor J. E. Charles will not be held liable or responsible for any consequences that come as a result of the actions taken based on reading the information contained herein. We do not claim to personally answer prayers; only Jesus Christ answers prayers, heals, and saves.

    The reader understands that no promises of success are made to the readers of this book. By reading this book you agree and understand that nothing said herein is meant to give medical, legal, or financial advice and should not be used in place of medical, legal, or financial advice from a qualified expert. If you are in need of legal, financial, or medical help, seek professional help and do not use the information in this book as a substitute for the guidance and advice of certified, qualified experts under any circumstances. Always be sure that you adhere to and obey the government, the laws, and the authorities of your country.

Contents

Introduction xi
   When the foundations are destroyed! xii
   Why is this book so important? xii
   It's time to wake up! xiii
   Deliverance is available today! xiv
   Think about this xiv

How To Use This Book xv

Part One

Chapter 1: Who is an Ancestor? 1
   Ancestral Practices in a New Age 2
   Evil Ancestral Powers 3
   Effects of Evil Ancestral Powers 5
   Family Tree 5
   What's a Family Tree? 6
   Some Biblical Insights into Family Tree 8
   Problems in the Family Tree 9
   Think about this 11
   Do this 12
   Prayer Points 12

Chapter 2: How are Evil Ancestral Strongholds and
Generational Bondage Formed?.. 14
    Blood Covenants.. 15
    Generational Bondage 15
    Satanic Seed – Satanic Tree – Satanic Fruit.................................... 16
    Cultural Ancestral Covenants... 17
    Divine Covenants 18
    Ancestral Covenants.. 19
    How People Enter into Evil Ancestral Covenants 20
    Think about this... 21
    Prayer Points... 21

Part Two: Dynamics of Deliverance from Ancestral Strongholds and Generational Bondage

Chapter 3: What is Deliverance?... 27
    Jesus Won the Battle to Give us Victory... 30
        A Person Made in God's Image 31
        A Person of Value and Dignity 31
    Salvation Prayer.. 32
    Affirmation of Your New Life in Christ.. 32
    Commencement Prayer 34
    False Prophets 34
    Think about this... 35
    Actionable Points 36
    Prayer Points... 36

Chapter 4: Attack by Evil Ancestral Powers through
Our Father's Lineage... 37
    Attack by Ancestral Powers.. 37
    Dealing with the Idols of our Father's House................................ 38
    Symptoms of Attack by Ancestral Powers 41
    How to Break Ancestral Powers and Attacks............................... 42
    Think about this... 42
    Prayer Points for Deliverance from Evil Ancestral Attacks......... 43

Chapter 5: How to be Free from Bitterness 45
Spot the Bug 47
What's in Your Heart? 51
How then do you renew your mind? 53
House the word in your Heart 53
Stand on Bended Knees 54
Let It Go! 56
God First Forgave You 56
Now It's Your Turn! 57
Stay Allied to Sweetness 59
Have a Support System 62
Prayer Points 63

Chapter 6: Breaking the Evil Ancestral Grip on Your Destiny 65
Ancestral Weapons 66
Spiritual Weapons 66
God's Word 67
Prayer 67
Fasting 68
Thanksgiving 68
The Armor of God 68
Think about this 71
Prayers to Break the Evil Ancestral Grip on Your Destiny 71

Chapter 7: Breaking Family Curses 73
What is a curse? 73
Family Curses 74
Think about this 77
Pray Points 78

Chapter 8: Liberation from Evil Garments 79
Examples of Evil Garments 80
Deliverance from Evil Ancestral Garments 81
Joshua he High Priest: Tainted with a Filthy Garment 81
Joseph: Adorned with a Coat Of Many Colors 82
Blind Bartimaeus: Garment of Sorrow 83
Ruth: A Change of Raiment 83

    God's Promise of a Garment Exchange 84
    Think about this 84
    Prayer Points for Removing and Destroying Evil Garments 85

Chapter 9: The Power and Place of Thanksgiving in Deliverance 86
    Thanksgiving to the Lord 86
        It is Right 86
        It is Powerful 87
        It Changes Our Heart 87
    Choose Thanksgiving! 88
    Think about this 88
    Actionable points 88
    Prayer Points for Thanksgiving to the Lord 89

Chapter 10: Engaging the Scriptures for Victory 91
    The Power of the Word 92
        An Unfailing Weapon 92
        A Weapon that Requires Training 92
        A Weapon Carried with Honor 93
    The Power is Available to You 93
    Think about this 94
    Action point 94
    Pray Points 94

Chapter 11: Scriptural Teachings and Prayers 96
    Asking God in Prayer 96
    God's Promises 97
    Think about this 98
    Declarations 98
    Prayer Points for Deliverance from Evil Ancestral Spirits 99

Chapter 12: How to Heal Your Poisoned Family Tree 101
    Examples from History 102
    A Poisoned Family Tree 102
    How to Heal Your Family Tree 104
        Understand Your Victory In Christ! 104
        Pray! 105

Renounce And Be Refined 106
Seek The Prophet's Intervention.. 107
Prayer 108

Chapter 13: Aggressive Prayer Based on the Scriptures.................... 109
Aggressive Prayer 110
Hannah 110
The Widow 110
Jesus 111
The Church and Peter 111
Aggressive Prayer Based on Scripture 111
Instances When You Need Deliverance 113
Ancestral Witchcraft.. 113
Eternal Safety in Christ 114
Think about this 115
Prayer Points for Deliverance from Ancestral
Witchcraft Powers 115

Chapter 14: Prayers for Revoking and Severing Soul Ties and Contracts 117
Soul Ties.. 117
Revoking Ancestral Vows, Pledges, Oaths, and Promises........... 118
Affirmations of Freedom in Christ.................................... 119
Revoking Soul Contracts 121
Declarations 124

Author Information 125

More books from J.E Charles... 127

Introduction

> *"In those days they shall say no more, the fathers have eaten a sour grape, and the children's teeth are set on edge."*
> **Jeremiah 31:29**

The most famous sermon in American history is "Sinners in the Hands of an Angry God," preached by Jonathan Edwards in 1741. So convicted were the people who heard it that they moaned aloud and cried out repeatedly, "What shall I do to be saved?" The sermon is credited with playing a part in sparking the First Great Awakening on American soil, which in turn is credited with inspiring the American Revolution and the founding of the United States.

Edwards and his wife had 11 children. Some years ago, a study was made of Edwards' male descendants, and here is what was found: More than 300 became pastors, missionaries, or theological professors. About 120 became professors at various colleges. About 110 became attorneys. Some 60 were prominent authors, 30 were judges, 14 served as presidents of universities and colleges, three served in the U. S. Congress, and one became vice-president of the United States.

All from this one faithful man.

Such is the importance of a family tree!

Ancestral powers and bondages are negative influences from the past—inherited from a poisoned family tree—that haunt us today and ruin our chances of a glorious tomorrow. The first step to a glorious future is to find freedom today from past mistakes and negative influences.

This is why I believe; this is not the time to live in ignorance. I maintain that everyone needs to be empowered to rise beyond the imposed limitations into new levels of power and opportunities. This is not the time to feel helpless; it's the time to gain wisdom and pull down the forces that might want to tie you down in the pit of your past. You can prosper beyond the limitations binding you, if you ensure that your spirit-man is liberated.

When the foundations are destroyed!

"If the foundation is destroyed, what can the righteous do?" - **Psalms 11:3**

Have you ever asked yourself why you find it hard to finish a good project? Do you wonder why those who could help you fulfill your destiny dissociate themselves from you? Have you ever sat down to question why you are unable to make progress despite the effort you put into life?

Almost everyone has wondered why there's a recurring pattern of negative occurrences along the family lines. Perhaps you are a third- or fourth-generation witness of a particular pain, ceaseless suffering, and trans-generational curse.

This book has answers to some of the mysteries of your life. By understanding ancestry and ancestral powers, you'll be equipped to detect and empowered to counter every negative ancestral influence over your life.

Why is this book so important?

Ancestral powers don't have respect for one's personality. When ancestral powers begin operation, your friend cannot help you. Ancestral power is not gentle; it is very violent; it embarrasses and mistreats one.

The operation of ancestral power can make one bitter. Wealth and education are not security against this satanic power. Ancestral power can destroy riches, connections, and render one's certificates useless. It causes sickness that can never be diagnosed. Ancestral power is destructive and ruthless.

It takes deep wisdom and strategic prayers to deal with critical problems in our lives. I like to say, "Pray today, so that you will not have to pray emergency prayers tomorrow." You have to arise from your spiritual sleep to wage war against forces that have monitored your ancestry for evil until now.

"The LORD is a man of war: the LORD is his name" -**Exodus 15:3**

God is not a civilian; rather, God is a soldier. This book is meant to permanently disconnect you from the operations of ancestral power by the power in the blood of the Lamb.

It's time to wake up!

For many years, the issue of deliverance was a silent topic in the church. Many believers never saw the need for deliverance, and many could not even entertain the thought of generational bondage.

Scripture, however, was not silent about the reality of the phenomenon of generational bondage. Obadiah revealed that *"upon mount Zion (the hill of the Lord), there shall be deliverance and the house of Israel (the people of God) shall possess their possessions"* (Obadiah 1:17).

The prophet Zechariah in a vision of the Lord also recorded that *"I raised my eyes and looked, and there were four horns. And I said to the angel who talked with me, 'What are these?' So he answered me, 'these are the horns that have scattered Judah, Israel, and Jerusalem. And I said, "What are these coming to do?' So he said, 'these are the horns that scattered Judah,* **so that no one could lift up his head***"* (Zechariah 1:18-19, 21, emphasis added).

The horns referred to in the above scriptures, which ensured that no one from Judah could lift his head, can be likened to ancestral strongholds. For in the same vein, there are ancestral powers today holding people down in a pit of undesirable, evil patterns in their lives.

Deliverance is available today!

In light of recent events, the subject of deliverance has gained wide prominence in the church and among believers. This is because many have been plagued with issues that have called for a focus on the subject of deliverance. The reality now stares us in the face that family and generational bondage does exist.

Ancestral issues reveal themselves in the form of negative patterns or occurrences within particular families or communities. Generational strongholds can also be seen as bloodline transfers, possibly from disastrous parental transactions with the enemy. From Scripture, we see an array of events that display this phenomenon.

With a well-detailed layout of the subject matter and a deep exposition into what generational bondage is and how to break free from it, this book will arm you with the wealth of knowledge needed to live out the life of victory Jesus has obtained for you. Are you ready?

Think about this:

Consider these powerful words from *The Minds Journal*:
It's up to us to break generational curses.
When they say, "it runs in the family," you tell them, "this is where it runs out."
Seeing unhealthy patterns in your family and deciding that those patterns end with you and will not be passed down to future generations is an extremely brave and powerful decision."[1]

---

[1] It's up to us to break generational curses when they say. https://themindsjournal.com/its-up-to-us/

How To Use This Book

With an abundance of inspired prayers, declarations, and affirmations, this book will take you through a step-by-step spiritual strategy to break free from every ancestral bondage and stronghold in your life.

To get the maximum benefit from this book, be ready to do the following:

1. Read and study the book prayerfully.

"And you shall know the truth, and the truth shall make you free." -**John 8.32**

Every bit of truth contained in the book is meant to facilitate your dissociation from every ancestral power holding you down. So, as you read, ensure that you are not taking a casual, religious or theoretical approach towards the book.

The deep truths embedded in the book can only be mined out when you set your heart to seek the truth. Remember, deep calls unto deep. As you engage in a meticulous study of the book, be prepared to receive your deliverance.

2. Engage the prayers violently.

"And from the days of John the Baptist until now the kingdom of heaven suffers violence, and the violent take it by force." -**Matthew 11:12**

Contained in every chapter of the book are powerful prayers, declarations, and affirmations. These prayers are to be said as instructed. Note that it's up to you to harness the power of prayer to deliver yourself from the ancestral chains holding you down.

"Deliver yourself like a gazelle from the hand of the hunter, and like a bird from the hand of the fowler." -**Proverbs 6:5**

One of the surest ways to free yourself from the bands of wickedness is by engaging in the fiery, powerful deliverance prayers listed. Pray these prayers like your life depends on it because it does.

3. Adhere to the instructions given.

"So Samuel said: 'Has the LORD as great delight in burnt offerings and sacrifices, As in obeying the voice of the LORD? Behold, to obey is better than sacrifice, And to heed than the fat of rams." -**1 Samuel 15:22**

One of the important elements of deliverance is prompt obedience to instructions. As you go through the pages of this book, there are various instructions laid out on things you need to do. These instructions are not merely a result of our feelings or thoughts. Rather, they are Spirit-birthed and offshoots of practical experience. As Mary said of her Son, *"Whatsoever he saith unto you, do it"* (John 2:5), so these instructions must be obeyed to yield fruit. Treat them as though they are proceeding directly from the mouth of the Lord Himself.

If the following have become the order of the day in your life, then you will find this book extremely useful in permanently solving your problems:

- Regular scary dreams and nightmares
- Finding yourself in ungodly relationships
- Strange movements in the body
- Emotional crises
- A life that is stuck and tied to a spot
- Hearing strange voices from unseen beings
- Operating under evil ancestral covenants and curses
- Suffering from unexplainable family breakdowns

- Constant attacks by evil spirits
- Consultations with witches for spells or enchantments
- Oppression and torment
- Rising and falling
- Unexplainable poverty
- Evil patterns in the family
- Profitless hard work
- Misfortunes
- Unpardonable errors and mistakes
- Infertility
- Late and wrong marriage

Regardless of your depth in the pit of ancestral curses, this book will only be profitable for you if you:

- Repent from and deal with every known sin - Psalm 51
- Surrender your life to Jesus - Acts 3:19
- Break evil covenants - Colossians 2:14-15
- Break evil curses attached to the covenants - Galatians 3:13-14
- Fast and pray your way to deliverance
- Pray recovery prayers - Joel 2:25
- Saturate your life with the blood of Jesus - Revelation 12:11

The Bible asks in Psalm 11:3, *"If the foundations be destroyed, what can the righteous do?"* The answer is: The righteous will pray!

It's time to claim your deliverance in Christ Jesus!

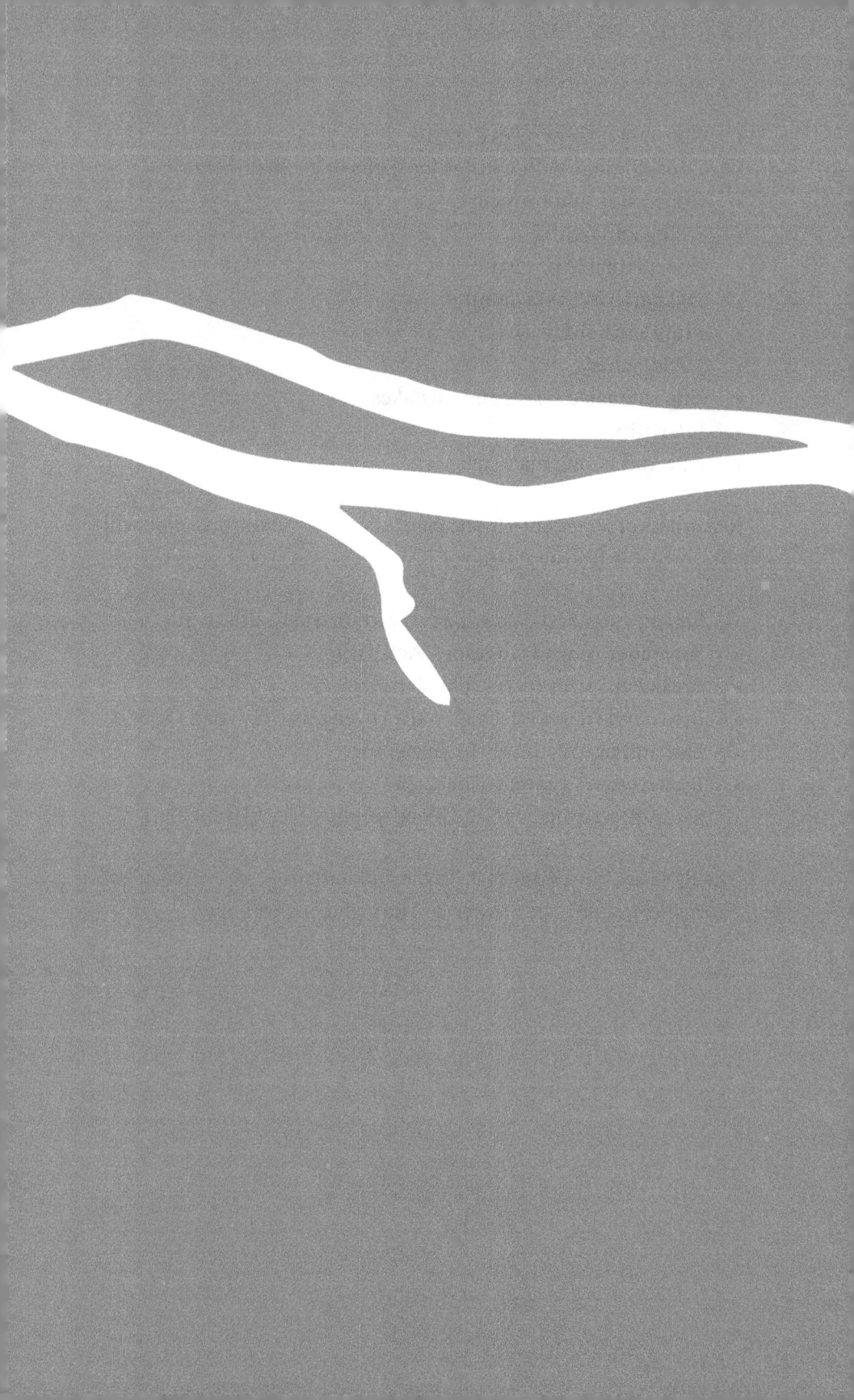

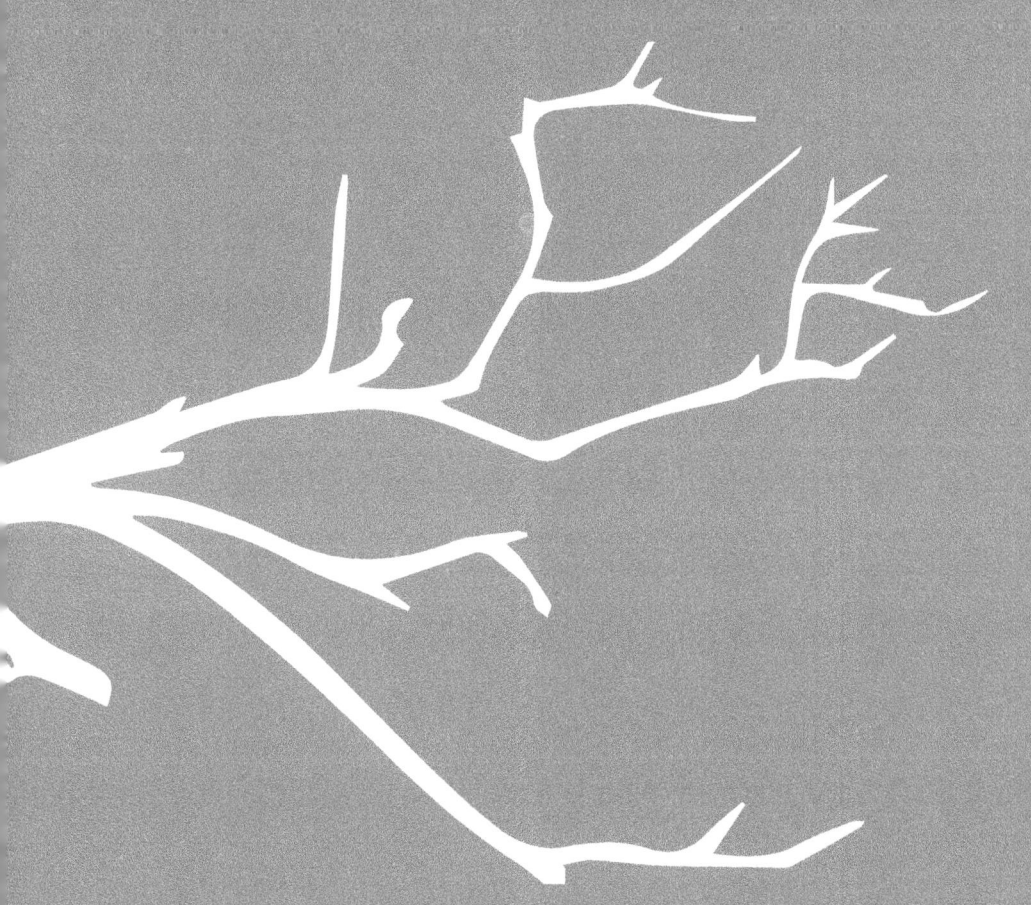

Part One

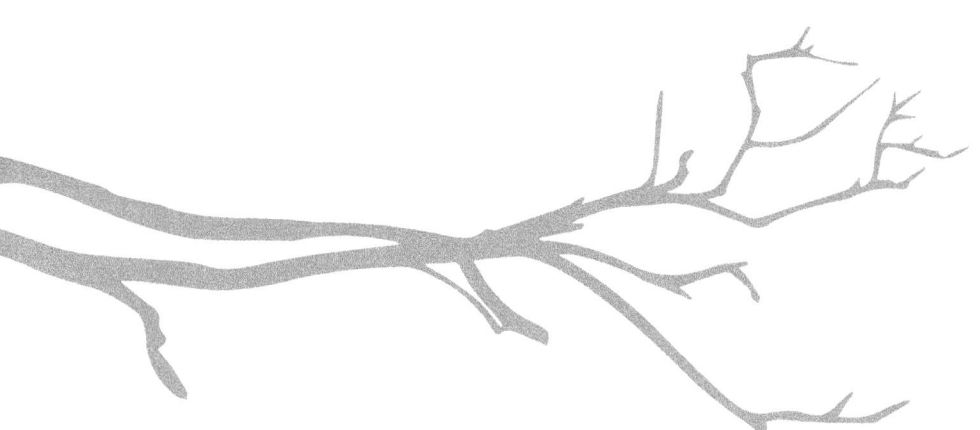

CHAPTER ONE

Who is an Ancestor?

The longest boxing match in history took place in New Orleans on April 6-7, 1893. It was fought between Andy Bowen and Jack Burke. It lasted 110 rounds and took 7 hours and 19 minutes—and ended in a draw. That's a long fight, beloved, but our spiritual battle with Satan has lasted a lot longer—and it won't end in a draw. We will either overcome in Jesus' power, or be overcome.

We must have wisdom for this battle, as Hosea 4:6 says, *"My people are destroyed for lack of knowledge."* Many people suffer frustration, defeat, or even death because they approach this battle of life with careless ignorance.

One truth we must understand is that our family tree—our ancestry—can be a weapon in the enemy's hand to set a curse in motion in our lives and family. Unfortunately, most of our ancestors did not know God; they served idols. As a result, many of their innocent descendants, though they do not worship those same idols, have become the enemy's legal captives through the promises, curses, and vows that their ancestors made to him and his agents by way of those idols. Multitudes of children, grandchildren, and great-grandchildren are in bondage due to a poisoned family tree.

The ancestors worshipped, served, and sacrificed foods like bananas, kola nuts, roasted corn, coconut, and wine to their gods. Doing this, they hoped for their desires to be met by these gods, as they passionately promised their posterity to them. In the heat of the moment, they inadvertently acquired and transmitted curses to unborn generations, selling them into slavery to ruthless deities.

Unfortunately, calamities flow through various families today due to the inputs of the ancestors. Several generations later, many in the family tree have become exposed to the only true and living God, and so have forsaken the brass, wooden, or golden gods in honor of their Creator.

Those of us who have joined our hearts to our Creator—God—have received a new and a better ancestral line. While our physical ancestors may have kidnapped and sold other humans and heaped curses on themselves, at salvation we believers swapped ancestral lines, replacing our physical ancestry with a new spiritual ancestry. Historically, the wave of change surged after the coming of Western Civilization. And many more are diving into that new spiritual ancestry every day!

Since the ancestors knew nothing about the saving gospel of Jesus Christ, they suffered and groped in darkness. But now, their children have received light for deliverance in Christ's name.

The onus is placed on younger generations who have experienced God's mercies to extend it to the older generations. This is because the older generations are still stuck in the rut of ancient practices that continue to transmit generational poverty, failure, disappointments, terminal illnesses, suffering, and lack of marriage.

Ancestral Practices in a New Age

"The habits that took years to build, do not take a day to change." - Susan Powter

Taking part in hideous acts became the habit of the older generations. They were used to performing evil rituals like visiting the graveyard and sleeping in the grave. Also, they burned incense, candles, chanted, and invoked evil powers. They ate flesh and drank libations and traditional brews to get high.

To note that these putrid practices have crept into churches is quite a surprise! Some got to the extent of allowing people to practice witchcraft, even in the church. No wonder that many churches today think it is okay to do such rituals in the church of God, denying holiness.

Some pastors even engage some people to do rituals for them before standing in the pulpit to preach. For example, the burning of candles, killing a goat, or killing a chicken. All of these stem from ancestral worship, and there are consequences as God prohibits such acts of impurity. To God, it is an abomination. (Exodus 20:3)

Evil Ancestral Powers

Ancestral powers are the powers of your foundation. They are the evil powers residing in a person's life. Ancestral powers usually sponsor family problems from one generation to another, in the same family bloodline. For as long as you are a member of that lineage, you might share with them in whatever happens. There are different ways of summoning these ancestral powers, e.g., using kola nuts, roasted corn, or cooking spices in graveyards, and these strange beings have certain foods that they eat once summoned. When the ancestral covenants are broken, it causes sanction or lays a siege upon the defaulter's life and his lineage.

Evil spirits and principalities are normally most active in the early hours of the day between 12 a.m. to 4 a.m. There are ancestral monitors that ancestral spirits use for surveillance over the lives of unsuspecting family members, and one of these is called Evil Global Positioning Systems (Evil-GPS). Suppose a family is from the marine kingdom. In that case, the ancestral power is predominantly put on the left leg, so anywhere a family member goes, they can be located, monitored, and seen in real-time.

Some other methods include putting tattoos and incisions on the body of the victim for marking and monitoring. Family idols may include things such as cows, crocodiles, alligators, or serpents. Ancestral powers use evil dedication and evil initiation to suppress their victims. When doing the initiation ritual, the victim is dedicated to a family idol, e.g., a serpent, cow, crocodile, or an alligator.

It is important to note that not all ancestral strongholds are evil. The agenda of the evil ancestral powers is as follows:

- They marry off family members to family idols, including serpents, marine idols, and marine spirits.
- They divert and confuse the destinies of their victims.
- They constantly monitor and survey the lives of targeted family members.
- Evil ancestral powers use the mediums of incisions, evil transmissions, tattoos, evil spiritual marks, tribal marks, or satanic GPS to monitor people's lives.
- They tend to manipulate people's lives more through their dreams, making enemies look like friends and friends like enemies.

Ancestral powers have powerful mediums of surveillance. If you always see a dog, cat, or big cats like leopards or tigers in your dreams, then you should know you are dealing with dangerous evil ancestral powers that are constantly monitoring your life.

Ancestral powers use evil dedication to family and village idols to keep their victims in perpetual bondage. These victims are dedicated to serpents, cows, goats, crocodiles, alligators, water demons, and water spirits. (Numbers 6:27, 25:3-5).

Evil ancestral powers have investments in your life through benefits that your ancestors obtained from them in the past, and it can even be thousands of years before you were born. Your life may have been used as collateral for these benefits. These benefits may include good health, the ability to have children, victory in various wars, a good harvest of crops, safety, and protection.

Your family may have sold you off to the spirit realm by marriage to spirits. And a time will come when you'll have to keep the terms of the agreement by offering sacrifices consistently. Thus, your ancestors mortgaged your life to these terrible powers.

Ancestral spirits operate in the realms of the heavens, earth, and water. If you are African, most times, the altar is in the sea. For Indians, the altars are in the earth; for Asians, the altars are in the heavens; and for Caucasians, most times, the altar is in a fire. A family priest usually oversees these altars. The altars continue to exist unless destroyed by the power of God.

Effects of Evil Ancestral Powers

- Mental illness.
- Delay in childbearing and infertility.
- Premature death.
- Sickness and affliction.
- Chronic poverty.
- Disaster.
- Sudden death.
- Calamity.
- Barrenness and madness.

Family Tree

1. Go back within the last four generations, in your family line, if possible, especially your grandparents, to obtain facts.
2. Carefully write down facts, traits, thoughts, patterns, memories, bad characteristics, problem areas, afflictions, and curses about living or dead relatives in your family line.
3. Make an inventory of your family generational problems. For example, issues listed could be untimely death, idolatry, incest, marital failure, polygamy, whoredom, occultism, anger, inherited diseases, etc.
4. Make a special offering to revoke evil ancestral vows binding you and limiting you, establishing a lasting covenant with Elohim. Luke 2:22 describes the laws of purification and offering unto Elohim to enter and revoke all evil vows. Be conscious and remember Psalm 74:20: *"Have respect unto the covenant:*

for the dark places of the earth are full of the habitations of cruelty."
5. Please allow yourself to be calm and focused.
6. Observe the Law of one "I AM" in your prayers.
7. Pray with all your body, soul, and spirit. Matthew 22:37, Revelation 1:8. Your speech, thoughts, imagination, mind, consciousness, heart, spirit, and body must be one.
8. All prayers must be prayed through —Jesus Christ.
9. Only Jesus can heal and save. We do not claim to answer prayers.
10. Pray with boldness in Jesus Christ's name.
11. All prayers of affirmations must be vocally proclaimed.
12. Possess your possessions and thank the Lord for answering your prayers.

What's a Family Tree?

According to research, a family tree is defined as a chart that maps a particular person's lineage for as far back as possible. A family tree can begin with the current generation and be traced backward. It could also start with the older generation and be traced forwards. It is a record of your lineage, showing your family members throughout recent and even distant history.

A family tree tells you who your family is, how it has grown and where you originally came from. There's more to a family tree than a chart of our lineage. It can tell a lot about why, how, and what we do today. Understanding the origin of your ancestors can help you answer a lot of questions about yourself.

Establishing and knowing your family tree can be tedious and time-consuming. The family tree can also be referred to as your ancestry, genealogy, bloodline, descent, lineage, pedigree, descendants, forebears, forefathers, foremothers, origin, ancestral tree, dynasty, genealogy charts, genealogy tree, paternity, family line, relatives, relations, offspring, genetics, maternity, family background, kith, kin, and in-laws.

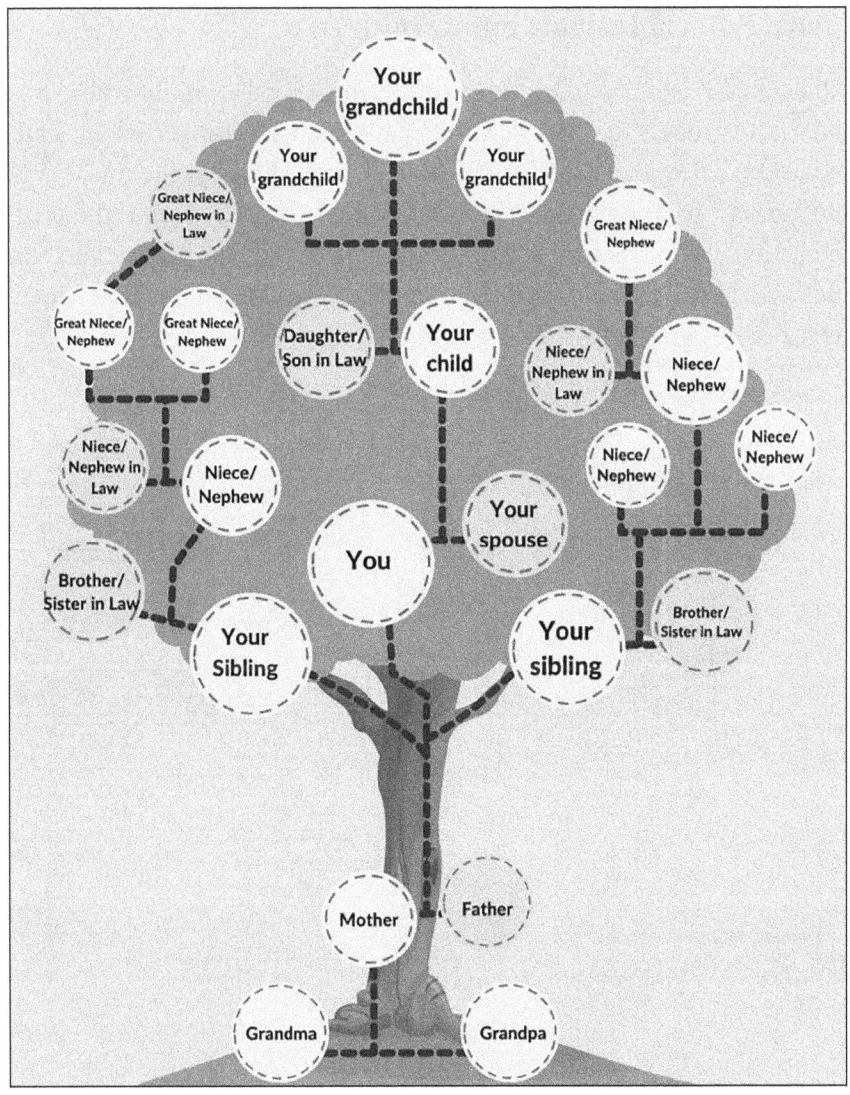

As you can see in the diagram, the family tree roots are grandmother and grandfather. Then, the stem that is directly attached to the grandparents is *the mother*. Thus, 90% of a human being's problems usually come from the mother's side. Then after the mother, it is the father. The father accounts for around 70% of the family problems. After your parents, the family tree elongates to you and your siblings up to your grandchildren.

Some Biblical Insights into Family Tree

The Bible has various insights and examples of a family tree. From Genesis through Revelation, God highlighted several genealogies and ancestral lineages. Genesis chapters 4, 5, and 11 report the lineal male descent to Abraham. Cain's genealogy is given in Chapter 4, the genealogy of Seth in Chapter 5, and Chapter 10 records the generations that descended from Noah. This shows that our God is meticulously interested in our genealogy (family tree).

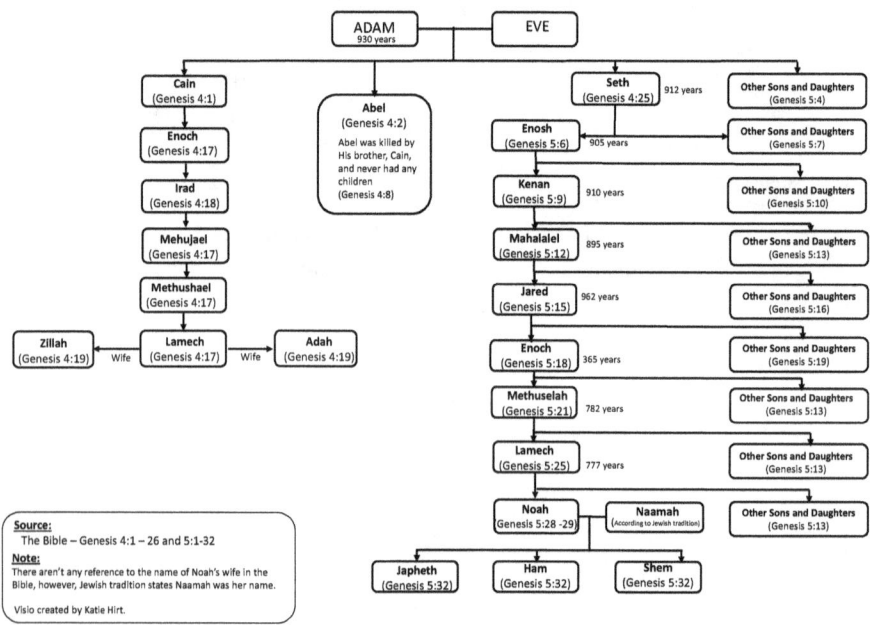

From the family tree above, it can be noted that there was a clear distinction between the descendants and genealogy of Cain compared with Seth's genealogy. Cain went against God when he killed Abel, his brother, and by so doing, he incurred a curse on himself, which eventually spanned through his descendants.

Going to the New Testament, Scripture reveals to us the family tree of Jesus. This was recorded in two of the Gospels—Matthew and Luke. The genealogy of Jesus dates as far back as the time of Adam. From the genealogy of Jesus, we understand that God deliberately chose and ordered the family from which Jesus was to come from. He couldn't be a descendant of Cain because of the prevalent curse in Cain's lineage, and so, he had to come from the line of Seth.

At times, the Israelites mingled with other people and indulged in their practices such as idol worship and immorality. Likewise, some of our ancestors also got involved in idol worship, and subsequent generations felt the effects of their practices. Just like God saved the Israelites from the Egyptians' grip, it is only God that can save us from our enemies and evil bondage. God abhors sin, and he punishes those who forsake his teachings and refuse to show remorse and repent.

We become clean in the Lord through abiding in him and obeying Christ's teachings. In life, we cannot succeed on our own, but rather we need God's mercy and guidance. When you are born again, you become a branch—a descendant—of Jesus Christ.

Problems in the Family Tree

Glitches in family trees are felt in many generations: past ones and those to come. Old Testament Israel understood this principle, as illustrated by the popular proverb referred to in Ezekiel 18:2: *"The fathers have eaten sour grapes, and the children's teeth are set on edge?"* Old Testament believers understood that one man's wickedness can bring suffering to all his lineage.

This principle is not only seen in the Bible, but in contemporary living as well. Consider this story:

Robert's parents divorced when he was just a little boy. Robert's father worked for many years as a pimp; he was notorious for prostituting and abusing women and when Robert was at the tender age of eight, his father committed suicide.

When Robert turned 14, he started his very own street gang, which quickly became known for its vicious violence and horrendous crimes of hatred and brutality. At 16 years old, Robert was sentenced to two years in prison for committing three drive-by shootings and armed robbery. The day he left for prison, his mother was brutally murdered by a rival street gang seeking revenge. Three-and-a-half- months later, his stepfather was gunned down by that same street gang. In prison, Robert was introduced to ruthless criminals worse than himself and his bent toward fighting and violence caused him to constantly be in and out of trouble.

Someone decided to search Robert's family tree and they discovered that Robert came from generations of folks who practiced destructive and violent behavior. Robert being younger and wiser than they, not only perpetuated this destructive behavior, but he took it to a whole new level.

Here is an example from the Bible of a problem in the family tree being passed down:

- Abraham told king Abimelech a lie that Sarah was not his wife.
- 40 years later, Isaac told the same lie that Rebecca was not his wife.
- 60 years later, Jacob's mother deceived Isaac.
- 80 years later, Laban deceived Jacob.
- 100 years later, Jacob, who deceived his father, was also deceived by his children.
- 120 years later, Reuben slept with his father's wife.
- 140 years later, Judah slept with his daughter-in-law.
- Many years later, Judas from the tribe of Judah betrayed Jesus.
- Reuben committed sexual abomination with his father's wife.
- Jacob's wife was the first woman to die during childbearing.
- Abraham slept with his wife's maid and sent her into the wilderness and many of the terrible wars and tragedies in the world today are due to this episode.

The devil always schemes to transmit evil from one generation to another. You must not allow him to succeed in his evil plans. This can only be done by giving your life to Jesus Christ and seeking deliverance from him.

Some of the common family problems experienced today are:
- Collective captivity.
- Unexplained hatred.
- Mysterious disease.

- Disappointment.
- Strange backward pressure.
- Reaping failure in the face of success.
- Horrible and terrible defeat in dreams.
- Consistent frustrations.
- The spirit of "grace to grass."
- The spirit of "going about in a circle."
- Abject poverty.
- Automatic failure mechanisms.
- Tragedies.
- Unhindered demonic activities.
- Disfavor.
- Unexplainable health failures.
- Academic frustration.
- Joblessness.
- Loss of virtues.
- Vagabond lives.
- Building but not living therein.
- Marital failure.
- Spirit of suicide.
- Merciless devotions.
- Witchcraft magnet. The person is just magnetizing witches. For instance, when they employ housemaid, they magnetize witchcraft.
- Acidic hardship.
- Old age suffering.
- Strange accidents.
- Going to the enemy for help. They approach witchdoctors for help.
- Manipulation.
- Being bothered by dead spirits.

Think about this:

"Call unto me, and I will answer thee, and show thee great and mighty things, which thou knowest not." -**Jeremiah 33:3**

When facing family tree problems, we should call upon God to save us and even save us from evil attacks fashioned against us that we do not know about. Ancestral strongholds and idol worship make one guilty by association due to being born in that family.

Do this:

Sing the song below to invite the power of the Holy Ghost upon your life.

Holy Ghost Fire, Fire fall on me
Pentecost Fire, Fire fall on me
On the day of Pentecost, Fire fall on me
Holy Ghost Fire, Fire fall on me
Pentecost Fire, Fire fall on me
Like on the day of Pentecost, the fire fall on me
Like on the day of Pentecost, the fire fall on me
Holy Ghost Fire, Fire fall on me
Pentecost Fire, Fire fall on me
Like on the day of Pentecost, Fire fall on me
Like on the day of Pentecost, Fire fall on me

Prayer Points

Prayer these prayers fervently:

1. Father God, wipe out all ancestral lineage impurities in our family bloodlines, and may all ancestral covenants be shattered and broken in the mighty name of Jesus Christ.
2. I renounce all ancestral idol worship in the name of Jesus Christ.
3. I command every idol in my father's house to lose their hold over my life, in the name of Jesus Christ.
4. Every strong power of my father's house, die, in the name of Jesus Christ.
5. I silence the cry of the evil powers fashioned against me, in the name of Jesus Christ.

6. All penalties of the worship of evil powers upon my life, I wipe you off by the blood of Jesus Christ.
7. Holy Ghost fire, destroy all spiritual shrines of my father's house, in the name of Jesus Christ.
8. Oppressive plan of the evil powers of my father's house, perish by fire.
9. Let any blood crying for vengeance against my generation shut up by the blood of Jesus Christ.
10. Every power speaking against my destiny, scatter in the name of Jesus Christ.
11. I break all ancestral pacts between evil powers and my father's house in the name of Jesus Christ.

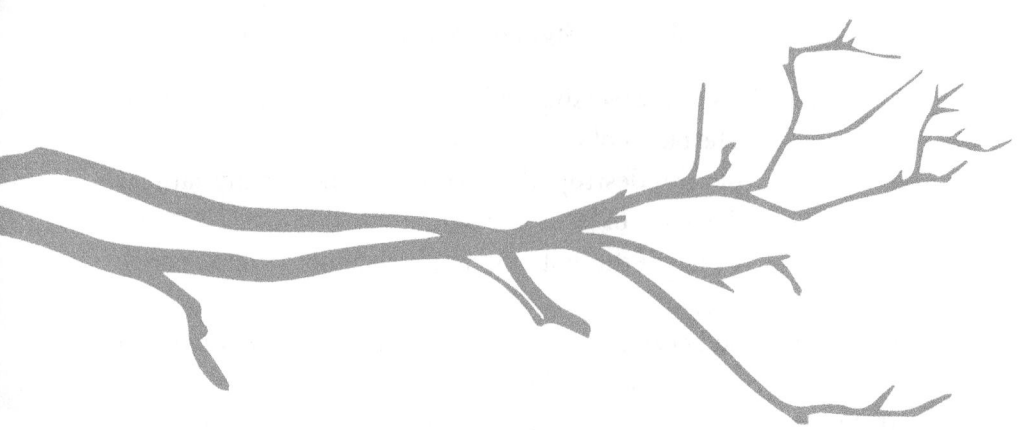

CHAPTER TWO

How are Evil Ancestral Strongholds and Generational Bondage Formed?

I n the 1980s, a young pastor moved to Whitewater, Wisconsin, to start a church and found it tough as nails, just like other Bible-believing churches had found it before his arrival. He did some research and learned that the town had a history of spiritism. A local resident named Morris Pratt had made a lot of money in iron ore on a tip from a medium in the 1800s, and so he had given himself to occultism and opened the Morris Pratt Institute—which became America's largest school of spiritism—right there in that town. In fact, the pastor's office was located in Pratt's old house. And *that,* the young pastor realized, was the source of his and other churches' difficulties, and the only cure was prayer! (*Church Planting Landmines,* pp. 101-102)

Beloved, the point is this: Past spiritual covenants can influence the present.

Blood Covenants

A covenant is a contract between two or more parties, in which they agree to fulfill promises, privileges, and responsibilities toward one another. From a biblical perspective, a covenant is a long-term deal or agreement that is binding on all parties involved and has dire consequences if broken or left unfulfilled.

Blood covenant involves using human or animal blood as a sign that all parties solemnly agree to their roles and responsibilities. Blood covenants, rituals, oaths, or promises are very strong and can have prolonged effects on someone or on generational lineage. There is only one blood that was shed to save us, which is the blood of Jesus Christ. You should pray against every blood that has spoken against you or your family lineage in the past.

To stop all ancestral covenants that cause calamities such as poverty, suffering, disappointments, and untimely death, one must break those covenants with the blood of Jesus Christ. Ancestral powers in your father's house can tie you to displaying perverted behavior and character, leading to the practice of immorality, prostitution, chronic fornication, stealing, and wickedness. Blood covenants can lead to the diversion and troubling of someone's good destiny.

Generational Bondage

Sandy is a committed Christian, who serves the Lord with her whole heart. She began to notice the symptoms of cancer of the pancreas. It was later confirmed by an abdominal CAT scan. The doctor told her that the scan showed what appeared to be a large tumor in her pancreas which was most likely malignant. She was scheduled to be admitted to the hospital the next day for surgery to biopsy the tumor to determine if it indeed was cancer. People with pancreatic cancer at that stage usually live only three to six months after receiving the diagnosis. There are no known effective treatments for this condition.

Sandy wasn't certain if it was God's will for her to live or die. She said, "I have been asking the Lord this very question. But, to be honest, I have so much pain, and my emotions are so involved—especially with my husband's terrible worry and grief—that I haven't been able to hear the Lord's answer clearly. However, deep inside, I just have this feeling that my work for Him isn't finished yet."

Sandy later said, "I have known for years that there is a curse of cancer on my family. As far back as I can trace, every member of my family has died from cancer at a fairly young age. Usually the cancer has been of the liver or pancreas. I thought I had broken the curse off of my own life, but now it looks like I have not been successful in doing so. I don't understand why. I should have the power in Christ to break it."[2]

Sandy and her family were suffering from generational bondage. Bondage is the state of being in captivity or enslavement involuntarily. *Generational* bondage refers to bondage that is passed down from one generation in a family to the next. It refers to an ancient authority in our father's or mother's house. It is also called ancestral bondage.

This ancient authority can affect human beings for a long time. It is a bad spirit that can be programmed into families through curses, dedication, bloodshed, worshipping of idols, etc. Ancestral bondage is a stubborn spirit that has been rooted in the family for many years. Deliverance from ancestral bondage requires rigorous prayers and fasting. It can be cured or broken through deliverance and the mercy of God.

Generational bondage can restrict people from moving forward or shining in life. This bondage in the ancestral lineage causes satanic counterattacks, setbacks, losses, deep poverty, untimely death, terminal diseases, chronic illness, delayed marriage, and robs people of their destinies. Just as the victims whose destinies have been stolen, those involved in stealing and diverting people's destinies also require rigorous deliverance.

Satanic Seed – Satanic Tree – Satanic Fruit

The devil is powerless in himself, but not foolish—he knows how to get us to use our own power, our own actions, against ourselves. That's why the Bible demands that we be vigilant. The way he works

---

[2] Page 19 of Unbroken Curses written by Rebbeca Brown.

is to plant seeds of perversion in the family line—such as immorality, anger, and murder—and then he watches as those seeds bear evil fruit.

As a believer, you must pray for the Holy Spirit to purge every seed the devil has planted in your life and that of your family members. You must rebuke every ancestral family altar and satanic obstacle. And, you need to know that some of the destiny thieves could be close family relatives.

Some of the bad behaviors and character traits that people possess were planted in their lives as a seed when they were young. And now, that bad behavior is the fruit of that seed, destroying their lives and hindering their destiny. All these bad behaviors cause havoc in people's lives, stealing, destroying, or delaying their destinies. You might have to pass through many trials, but it will be better for you than others if you depend on Jesus Christ fully.

Cultural Ancestral Covenants

Many of our ancestors, though dead, are not resting in peace because there are people called "spirit drawers" that are always drawing energy from the dead. Those people have different religions in all parts of the world, including Africa and the Caribbean.

In the Caribbean, there is one tribe called Maya. Most Maya members today observe a religion composed of ancient Mayan ideas, animism, and some Catholicism. The Maya still believe that their original village or habitation is the center of the world supported at its four corners by gods. When one of these gods shifts its burden, they believe it causes an earthquake.

There is another sect called the "Blue draws." Mayism is where somebody can call an ancestor's name or someone that has passed away, and the person's spirit will appear. The spirit can enter into a walking human being and sometimes even have sexual intercourse spiritually or physically together and indulge in acts such as kissing the person. The spirit can also use the person's tongue to talk and pass a message to the living.

These are typical examples of the evil cultural ancestral spirits and covenants. Some communities summon the ancestral spirits through actions such as drums beating, offering foods or drinks, and when the spirit enters them, they will start to manifest. The devil has power, but Jesus Christ has more power, and he defeated the devil on the cross. Thus, such powers should not bother born again believers.

Abuse of drugs such as alcohol, cocaine, marijuana, and heroin is a pathway to inviting a foreign spirit into your life. No reasonable born again person should be addicted to drugs or alcohol as it opens pathways for the devil and his agents. Have respect for the covenant we have with Yahweh and the New Testament's covenant of the blood of the Lamb of God. It is very risky to combine two covenants.

You cannot claim to be born again and filled with the Holy Ghost while you are still drinking alcohol and conjuring evil spirits. No! you're either here or there. The Bible states clearly that no one can serve two masters at a time. So, you've got to choose which path you'll tread. The truth is, once you are born of God, and the Holy Spirit dwells in you, you should abstain from anything that can invite the devil into your life with evil spirits.

Anybody who has been investing his money and resources against the fire and word of the living God shall be destroyed in the name of Jesus Christ.

"Whoso diggeth a pit shall fall therein: and he that rolleth a stone, it will return upon him." -**Proverbs 26:27**

The thunder of the Lord will strike those enemies of the gospel who have been plotting evil against the believers. Amen. We have an assurance of answered prayers in Christ. The Psalmist had this confidence when he said: *"O thou that hearest prayer, unto thee shall all flesh come"* (Psalm 65:2).

Divine Covenants

To say something is divine means that it is related to, devoted to, or proceeds from God. Covenants that were made in the Bible are called divine covenants. Some examples of these covenants are God's covenant with Abraham, in which he promised Abraham that he would be the father of many nations; God's covenant with David, in which he promised that the Savior would come from his bloodline; and God's covenant with Noah, in which he promised that he would never destroy the earth again with water.

In the New Testament, there is the covenant with Jesus Christ whereby he died for the salvation of our souls, and whereby now the Law of God has been written in our hearts. These covenants were all spoken, hence, the strong relationship between covenants and word of mouth.

Ancestral Covenants

A covenant is an accepted agreement or decision between two or more people to establish a relationship that includes promises, responsibilities, and punishments for breaking the covenant. It is legally binding and irrevocable. In general, a covenant refers to any form of a pledge in written or oral form concluded between two or more persons. It can also entail a promise to perform or abstain from certain things or actions.

An ancestral covenant is a covenant formed and contracted by our forefathers, binding on everyone in that family. This covenant is irreversible, and only the blood of Jesus Christ can break it. Covenants are formed through word of mouth, and they may also include writing if necessary. Certain aspects are vital in forming a covenant. Those aspects include the naming of the people making the covenant, the reason or purpose of the covenant, the place where the covenant was made, word of mouth, and the consequences and punishments for breaking the covenant.

Some of the punishments for breaking a covenant may include sudden death, poverty, disaster, calamity, barrenness, and madness. It is your responsibility to investigate your family concerning any past covenants that your ancestors might have entered into and launch a vigorous prayer to destroy every evil covenant that was contracted in the past. Total deliverance is required to overcome the evil covenants and their liabilities. God commanded in Exodus 23:32-33:

"Thou shalt make no covenant with them, nor with their gods. They shall not dwell in thy land, lest they make thee sin against me: for if thou serve their gods, it will surely be a snare unto thee."

As you pray, you should break all soul ties and every evil covenant of idol worship made in the past that may affect your life and your family.

The art of entering into a covenant began with God. God made a covenant with Noah, Abraham, and David; also the New Testament covenant, which is still in operation today, was initiated by God. From this, we can see that God is a God of the covenant, and his word and promises always come to pass. He would not say what he does not mean. The Bible says, *"Heaven and earth shall pass away, but my words shall not pass away"* (Matthew 24:35). He is always watching his covenant. God's commitment to do anything is in a covenant.

How People Enter into Evil Ancestral Covenants

There are various ways by which people knowingly or unknowingly initiate and enter into an evil ancestral covenant. Some of these ways are:

- Sex outside marriage – The Bible in 1 Corinthians 6:16 says, *"What? know ye not that he which is joined to a harlot is one body? for two, saith he, shall be one flesh."* Many people have failed to recognize that sex is spiritual and that it is one of the legal ways a covenant can be easily initiated. This is because the crucial element needed for a covenant to be enacted is involved – blood.
- Pictures – Your pictures can be used to cast a spell or a charm on you.
- Through blood and body fluids such as semen; hair and nails; DNA
- Counterfeit religion or idol worship that entails performing ungodly rituals.
- Occult covenants – Joining sects such as prosperity clubs for earthly things, thereby swearing allegiance with your blood to never leave the group till death.

- Through food and drinks, the giving of which can be used to initiate people into witchcraft.
- Demonic fashions. For instance, rings, necklaces, clothing, shoes, and bracelets. Some of the materials used to make these items, like gold or diamonds, may have the symbolism of idolatry from the place they were manufactured.

Think about this:

The identity you carry can be used to manipulate and change your destiny. Through blood covenant and other forms of the covenant, you have been brought into the identity of your family. So, you're directly linked to anything going on in that family.

Prayer Points

1. Every bitter water flowing and affecting my family through my lineage, dry up in the name of Jesus Christ.
2. Any cord binding my family to my ancestors, break, in the name of Jesus Christ.
3. Every landlord spirit troubling my destiny, be paralyzed in Jesus's name.
4. Every outflow of a satanic family name, die, in the name of Jesus.
5. I recover all benefits stolen by my father's house's evil powers, in the name of Jesus.
6. Where is the Lord God of Elijah? Arise and disgrace every evil power of my father's house, in the name of Jesus.
7. Every devilish priest ministering in my family line, be removed in Jesus' name.
8. Darts of affliction originating from my lineage's idolatry, break, in the name of Jesus.
9. Every evil influence originating from my father's house and affecting my family, perish.
10. Every network of the evil powers in my place of birth, scatter in Jesus' mighty name.

11. Every Satanic dedication that speaks against me, be destroyed in the name of Jesus.
12. I vomit every food with an idolatrous influence that I have eaten, in the name of Jesus.
13. Every unconscious evil, internal altar, catch fire in the name of Jesus.
14. Every stone of hindrance from my father's house, be rolled away, in the name of Jesus.
15. Every part of my life being used to test diabolical weapons, be nullified by the blood of Jesus.
16. Shame, loss, discouragement, self-pity, pollution, evil odors, I am not your candidate. Go back to your senders in Jesus's name.
17. I nullify all the causes of delay and stagnation of my career and progress in life in the mighty name of Jesus.
18. Oh God, thank you in advance for my deliverance from ancestral covenants.
19. Father, I come before you and ask that you forgive my sins and that of my ancestors.
20. Every evil ancestral covenant and agreement reigning in my family and foundation, be revoked and canceled in Jesus's name.
21. Blood of Christ, destroy and revoke all evil covenants, vows, oaths, and promises in my life in Jesus' name.
22. I break every evil covenant of evil repetition in my family line working against me in the name of Jesus.
23. Every agent of darkness operating an evil covenant in my family line, be arrested by fire in the name of Jesus.
24. I nullify you, covenants of chains of problems functioning against my family and me, in the name of Jesus.
25. Every covenant of spirit of condemnation, confusion, and conflict that is destroying destinies and blessings in my family, I break you in the name of Jesus.
26. Every family altar and its covenants speaking against my life, I break, destroy and bind it in the name of Jesus.
27. I break all covenants and contracts that my father, mother, and ancestors entered into with the devil for help, gifts, protections, or any type of service or earthly possessions, in the name of Jesus.

28. I break down every stronghold of evil blood covenant in my life, in the name of Jesus.
29. I speak destruction into the root of uncleanness in my life, in the name of Jesus.
30. I withdraw my bloodline from every evil altar, in the name of Jesus.
31. Every stubborn evil altar priest, drink your own blood now, in the name of Jesus.
32. Lord, make everything the enemy has pronounced over me to be impossible, in the name of Jesus.
33. Any demon attached to any curse around my life, depart from me now, in the name of Jesus.

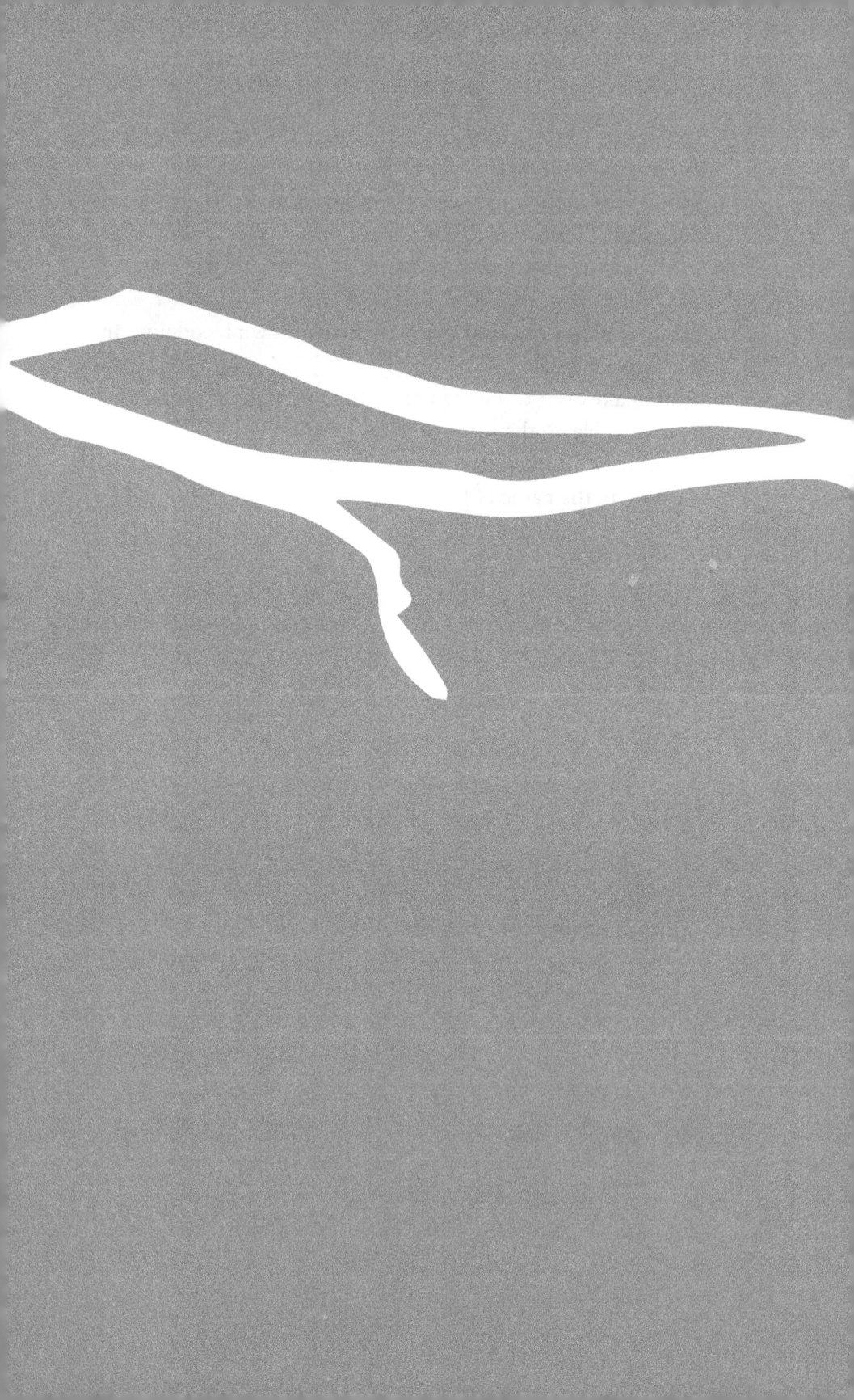

PART TWO

Dynamics of Deliverance from Ancestral Strongholds and Generational Bondage

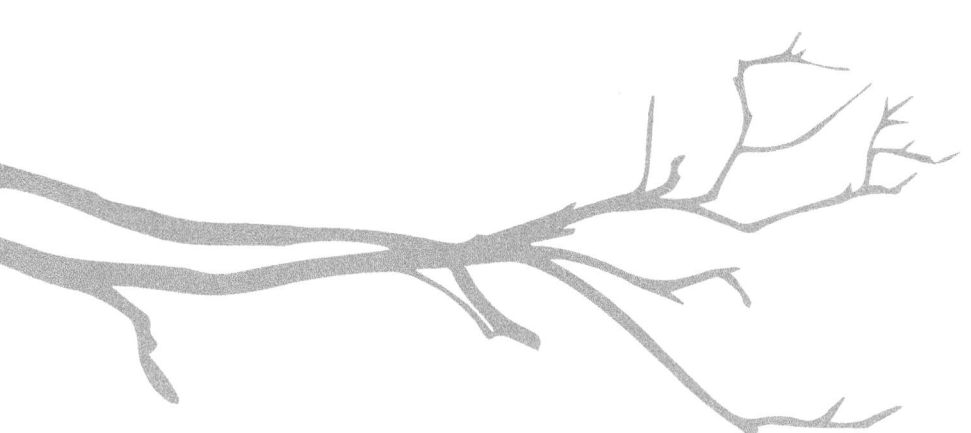

CHAPTER THREE

What is Deliverance?

In U. S. history, there was a certain man who failed in business in 1831. He was defeated for the Legislature in 1832. He failed again in business in 1833. He suffered a nervous breakdown in 1836. He was defeated for Speaker of the Legislature in 1838. He was defeated for Elector in 1840. He was defeated for Congress in 1843. He was defeated again for Congress in 1848. He was defeated for the Senate in 1855. He was defeated for Vice President in 1856. He was defeated for the Senate again in 1858....

Finally, this man who seemed to know nothing but defeat, was elected President of the United States in 1860 and proceeded to save the Union. This is, of course, the story of Abraham Lincoln, now almost universally considered America's greatest president. (Rick Joyner, *Leadership: the Power of a Creative Life*).

As with President Lincoln, the child of God—a Christian—is not immune to failure; he or she is still vulnerable to the enemy's attacks, he or she can still be violated and defeated by sin. But also like President Lincoln, defeat need not be final for the Christian! We have a God who will pick us up, dust us off, and set us on track again! Consider these comforting words by classic Christian author C. S. Lewis:

"I know all about the despair of overcoming chronic temptations. It is not serious provided self-offended petulance, annoyance at breaking records, impatience, etc., don't get the upper hand. No amount of falls will undo us if we keep on picking ourselves up each time. We shall, of course, be very muddy and tattered children by the tie we reach home. But the bathrooms are all ready, the towels put out, and the clean clothes in the airing cupboard. The only fatal thing is to lose one's temper and give it up. It is when we notice the death that God is most present in us: it is the very sign of His presence."

Just imagine it: Even stuck and sinking in the miry pit of sin, we can reach out for cleansing and be restored to the righteousness of God, to right-standing with him! While a believer may suffer oppression as result of their sin, God has a backup plan to deliver us each time we fall behind. Check out the following words as LeRoy Lawson as he expresses the mind of God for his children:

"One is a chosen child, a valued member of the family of God. God wants just the best for one, including power over the devil himself."

True! Believers may experience physical, psychological, spiritual, and emotional problems due to evil spirits' activities in their lives, but God wants us to prevail over the devil in all these areas of our life. He wants to deliver us from the prison house of the enemy, as the following story of deliverance from generational bondage reveals:

"Ann had been severely ritualistically abused from her early childhood until she left home at the age of nineteen. Ann is from one of the royal families of Europe. She told me that just before her mother's death she was given a number of items which she was instructed to guard carefully and then pass on to her own daughter. Her mother told Ann that she would die if she lost any of the articles or allowed them to be destroyed. When Ann asked her mother why the things she had been given were so important, she was told that they ensured the continuation of her family's power.

"This power comes from the demon spirits associated with the family. Her family had worshiped and served Satan for generations. In fact, Ann had an ornate family tree drawn on an old parchment that went back to the fifteenth century.

"This young woman was the first member of her family to accept Christ. Ann brought the items with her when she came to see me. She prayed over each one, breaking the lines of inheritance and any curses associated with them. As we burned each item, Ann commanded all the demons associated with the articles to leave her life forever in the name of Jesus Christ. The most interesting article was the certificate of citizenship given to her first ancestor who immigrated to the United States. It was dated 1850. Her mother had emphasized to Ann the great importance of this document to insure the continuance of power in her branch of the family that now lived in the U.S. We wondered why it was important, so we prayed and asked the Lord to reveal the reason to us. The Lord showed both of us at the same time. That certificate of citizenship was the legal doorway that allowed all the demons associated with her family line to have clear entrance into the United States! I had never thought of this idea before. As Ann burned the citizenship certificate of her ancestor, she not only commanded the demons out of her life, but also commanded all the demons associated with her family line to leave America forever. Then she asked the Lord to close that doorway so they could not return." [3]

In Christianity, deliverance refers to cleansing people of evil spirits and demons and setting them free through prayers. It is the act of being rescued or set free from internal and external bondage. And this is done to address and end the problems of demonic possession, thereby stopping their oppressive operations in people's lives.

Jesus Christ carried out both healing and deliverance on the people that came to him.

"The Spirit of the Lord is upon me because he hath anointed me to preach the gospel to the poor; he hath sent me to heal the brokenhearted, **to preach deliverance to the captives**, *and recovering of sight to the blind, to set at liberty them that are bruised"* (Luke 4:18, emphasis added).

This scripture reveals the course that Jesus' ministry would take. Jesus declared that one of the objectives of his ministry would be to bring deliverance to the captives. In his lifetime, Jesus worked deliverance for many who were oppressed by the devil. Below is an example of Jesus' deliverance model:

---

[3] Page 22 of Unbroken Curses by Rebecca Brown MD.

"And he came down with them, and stood in the plain, and the company of his disciples, and a great multitude of people out of all Judaea and Jerusalem, and from the sea coast of Tyre and Sidon, which came to hear him, and to be healed of their diseases; and they that were vexed with unclean spirits: and they were healed." -**Luke 6:17-18**

Christ advised many healed to become born again, follow his teachings and avoid backsliding into the same sin that led them into the problem they just got delivered from. This was so that the devil would regain no control over them at all.

"Afterward, Jesus findeth him in the temple, and said unto him, Behold, thou art made whole: **sin no more, lest a worse thing come unto thee.**" -**John 5:14, emphasis added.**

Such an instruction was necessary because one of the ways the devil gains entrance into people's lives is through their sinful acts. Therefore, when someone has been delivered from the oppression of the devil, such a person must be instructed not to go back to their sins lest the devil regain entrance into their life, making it worse than before. Jesus said:

"When the unclean spirit is gone out of a man, he walketh through dry places, seeking rest; and finding none, he saith, I will return unto my house whence I came out. And when he cometh, he findeth it swept and garnished. Then goeth he, and taketh to him seven other spirits more wicked than himself, and they enter in, and dwell there: and the last state of that man is worse than the first." -**Luke 11:24-26**

Jesus Won the Battle to Give us Victory

"And they overcame him by the blood of the lamb, and by the word of their testimony, and they loved not their lives unto death." -**Revelation 12:11**

On the cross, Jesus gave us dominion over the devil and his agents when he said, *"It is finished"* (John 19:30). Through the blood of Jesus, all believers are overcomers. We can overcome every satanic attack against our lives through the blood of the Lamb.

As Christians, we have been elevated into heavenly realms to reign with God. We have an unmatchable identity in Christ right from the beginning of the world. Let's take a moment to look over our uniqueness in God:

A Person Made in God's Image

Then God said, "Let us make mankind in our image, in our likeness, so that they may rule over the fish in the sea and the birds in the sky, over the livestock and all the wild animals, and over all the creatures that move along the ground."

So God created mankind in his own image, in the image of God he created them; male and female he created them. **-Genesis 1:26-27 (NIV)**

A Person of Value and Dignity

[15] The Lord God took the man and put him in the Garden of Eden to work it and take care of it. [16] And the Lord God commanded the man, "You are free to eat from any tree in the garden; [17] but you must not eat from the tree of the knowledge of good and evil, for when you eat from it you will certainly die."

[18] The Lord God said, "It is not good for the man to be alone. I will make a helper suitable for him."

[19] Now the Lord God had formed out of the ground all the wild animals and all the birds in the sky. He brought them to the man to see what he would name them; and whatever the man called each living creature, that was its name. [20] So the man gave names to all the livestock, the birds in the sky and all the wild animals.

But for Adam no suitable helper was found. [21] So the Lord God caused the man to fall into a deep sleep; and while he was sleeping, he took one of the man's ribs and then closed up the place with flesh. [22] Then the Lord God made a woman from the rib he had taken out of the man, and he brought her to the man.

[23] The man said, "This is now bone of my bones and flesh of my flesh; she shall be called 'woman,' for she was taken out of man."

[24] That is why a man leaves his father and mother and is united to his wife, and they become one flesh.

[25] Adam and his wife were both naked, and they felt no shame. **-Genesis 2:15-25 (NIV)**

See, no matter what you go through, have faith through the precious blood of Jesus that you shall overcome all challenges directed to you by the enemy. Why is that? It's because you are not ordinary!

Christians should ask God to increase their strength to overcome battles and setbacks in life. Most of the time, challenges are not a way of punishing us but rather a way to strengthen our faith in God.

"Finally; my brethren, be strong in the Lord; and in the power of his might. Put on the whole armor of God, that ye may able to stand against the wiles of the devil." -**Ephesians 6:10-11**

This verse reveals the believer's great confidence when it comes to spiritual warfare, namely, the strength and might of God. The Bible says that we should put on the whole armor of God to withstand all the fiery darts of the devil. Using the blood of Jesus Christ, you should draw a circle of protection around your dwelling place and your body, spirit, and soul. Never put your trust in yourself or man but rather rely solely on God who created heaven and earth.

Salvation Prayer

"Christ hath redeemed us from the curse of the law, being made a curse for us: for it is written, cursed is every one that hangeth on a tree." -**Galatians 3:13**

Pray this prayer with me to accept Jesus Christ as your Lord and Savior:

"Father in Heaven, I agree that I am a sinner (Romans 3:23). I come to you, Lord. As I speak, I have decided to leave my sinful ways and I ask that you make me clean by the blood of Jesus Christ. I believe that Jesus died on the cross to take my sins away. I also believe that he rose from the dead so that I will be redeemed and made righteous through faith in him (Romans 6:23). I surrender my life to Jesus Christ to be my Lord and Savior (Acts 2:21). I declare now that I am born again and a child of God (Romans 10:9-10). I am delivered from the grip of sin, and I am the expression of the righteousness of God. I am saved in Jesus' name, amen."

Affirmation of Your New Life in Christ

As a Christian, you have a new spiritual identity. Following are some faith affirmations, drawn from the Scriptures, that describe your new identity in God's eyes:

- ✓ I was dead in sin by natural inheritance, for I was brought forth and conceived in sin and iniquity right from my mother's womb. Going by the Law, I was marked out for the wrath of God that was to be revealed upon the children of disobedience, but now I am God's workmanship, recreated in Christ, born anew that I may do these good works which God already predestined for me.

- ✓ Through the blood of Jesus Christ, I, who was lost and far from God, have been brought near to God. I have now become deeply rooted in Christ my Messiah, and I have become a brand-new man. The lifestyles, the previous moral and spiritual condition that formed a part of my making, have passed away and I am now totally new, different from what anyone has seen or known before.

- ✓ Therefore, since I am declared the righteousness of God in Christ and have been given a right standing with God through faith, I have peace with God, having been justified by the blood of Christ, and he shall save me from the wrath that will fall on everyone that hasn't believed.

- ✓ The person becomes one spirit with God when he unites with him. Therefore, there is now no condemnation for those who are in Christ Jesus, who do not walk according to the desires of the flesh but according to the desires of the Spirit. For the Law that guides our new life, which is the Law of the fruits of the Spirit of Christ, has delivered me from the Law of sin and death. I am set apart by God through the liberation in the blood of Christ my Messiah, the Alpha and Omega of my faith, from every connection with ancestral covenants, curses, and monitoring spirits.

- ✓ I am now a citizen of Heaven. I belong to the household of God. My life is hidden with Christ in God. I am cleansed in the blood of him who loved me and gave his life for me, the one who called me by his name with a holy calling, leading to a life of consecration and vocation of holiness. I am now cut out and made separate from all evil consequences. I'm a new being in Christ Jesus, Amen.

The Law brought a curse, but the Christian is delivered from that curse. How? Through Jesus Christ who took it upon Himself to purchase the salvation of our souls on the cross. This huge sacrifice redeemed all human beings from the wrath of God.

Commencement Prayer

"O Lord, I pray against the evil mirror. May it shatter and break into pieces. Every eye of darkness that has been assigned against me, I smack it with the blood of Jesus. All my buried virtues are exhumed. Everything buried against me or representing me in the grave will be exhumed in the name of Jesus Christ. All my buried virtues, glory, marriage, career, and riches, come alive. I declare that all witchcraft embargo against my destiny, career, and success be lifted out of the way by the Holy Ghost's fire."

False Prophets

A prophet is a person who communicates God's will to the people. A prophet can discern what will occur in the future accurately. In biblical teachings, a false prophet is a person who falsely claims the gift of prophecy or divine inspiration to speak for God. A false prophet may do so for self-gain or evil purposes, such as intentionally diverting people from the truth.

In the last days, Jesus warned us, we should beware of false prophets who will come in sheep's clothing but inwardly they are ravenous wolves seeking to devour (Matthew 7:15). Jesus further warns that many will be led astray and deceived as the false prophets will have the ability to show great signs and wonders before the eyes of men (Mark 13:5-6).

One of the tricks of the false prophets is to deceive and trap. They lure in unsuspecting people and lead them astray like sheep to the slaughter. They trap their congregation, take their photo, build a soul tie with them and begin to work diabolical rituals on their victims. Falsehoods and a deceiving doctrine are the swords of a false prophet.

"The integrity of the upright shall guide them: but the perverseness of transgressors shall destroy them." -**Proverbs 11:3**

The Spirit of God is the guide for an upright man to follow, as the Spirit leads us to the truth and the path of righteousness. The Spirit of God helps us to overcome fleshly desires that lead us to the path of sin and unrighteousness.

"In the LORD, I put my trust: how say ye to my soul, Flee as a bird to your mountain? For, lo, the wicked bend their bow, they make ready their arrow upon the string that they may privily shoot at the upright in heart." -**Psalm 11:1-2**

"O, Lord! We apply the Law of boomerang: Any wicked man or woman who will bend and shoot an arrow towards the righteous, may it go back to him or her and their household. Lord, shield us from all the attacks of our enemies."

There is no guarantee that believers will not face difficult situations in life, but when they do, the righteous should always seek the face of Jesus, our help and victory during those troubling and tough times.

Think about this:

"And God saw that the wickedness of man was great in the earth and that every imagination of the thoughts of his heart was only evil continually." -**Genesis 6:5**

When God created all the things, he was impressed and said it was good. Years later, sin began to be predominant among the earth's inhabitants, and God was furious. Every sin committed by mankind was not a result of error, ignorance, or drifting from God, but rather it resulted from man's deliberate rejection of God. The increase of sin came at a cost as God reduced the average lifespan of human beings.

We do not only sin from our actions but also with our hearts and minds. After Adam and Eve were expelled from the Garden of Eden, the human race was accorded the freedom to choose God and follow his commandments or to choose Satan.

Actionable Points:

- If any man is in Christ, He's a new creature. Therefore, I surrender my life to Christ so that I can be immune from every evil dart of the enemy
- I decide to commit myself to feed on a true prophet of God so that I do not expose myself to evil men who are wolves in sheep's clothing.
- I remind myself every time and every day that through the finished work of Christ on the cross, I have become the righteousness of God in Christ Jesus, and I speak the word of God daily over everything that raises its ugly head against my life.

Prayer Points

1. I dip and shield myself properly with the blood of Jesus.
2. Every ancestral grip and evil consequences as a result of my forefather's idol worship, break by fire in the name of Jesus.
3. Every evil covenant with water spirits, witchcraft spirits, guardian spirits, and family gods, be broken now by the blood of Jesus.
4. Family, village, and serpentine spirits that made me inherit a spiritual wife/husband, be cast out in the mighty name of Jesus Christ.
5. I revoke and destroy all words, vows, and promises made against me to limit my future with the thunder of Jesus. I claim my purpose in Jesus' name.
6. I claim divine reinstatement of all that the devil has stolen from me and reclaim it multifold.
7. I break all agreements with all Dreamtime societies formed consciously and unconsciously.
8. I call forth all the evil copies, backup copies, reinstatement clauses, mirrors of the agreements, and render them null and void.
9. I am no longer a being and vessel of ancestral karma. All the debt that has been projected to me, I revoke and reverse it by the blood of Jesus, and I now return it to the sender.
10. Every legal ground that ancestral and guardian spirits have in my life, be destroyed by the blood of Jesus.

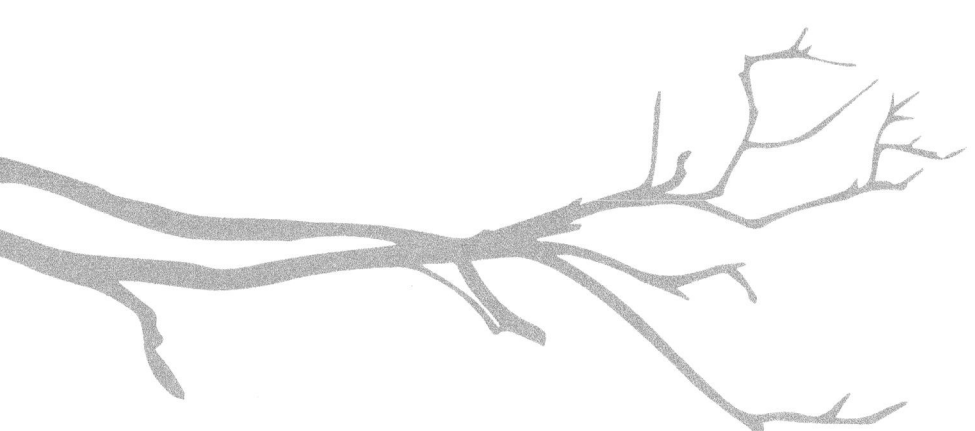

CHAPTER FOUR

Attack by Evil Ancestral Powers through Our Father's Lineage

A Christian psychologist told the story of 15-year-old Mary. A friend approached Mary and asked if she wanted a cigarette. Mary replied, "No thanks. We Craigs don't smoke." Mary's sense of belonging and identity to her family gave her healthy self-esteem, and she did not feel the need to compromise her standards to fit in with anyone else. (Dr. Kevin Leman, *Have a New Kid by Friday*. Names changed.)

Attack by Ancestral Powers

As mentioned earlier, not all ancestral powers are evil. There are good ancestral strongholds, such as that built up against smoking for 15-year-old Mary. But there are also evil ancestral powers. The evil ones do not have good intentions for a family. The agenda of evil ancestral powers from our father's house is to kill, steal, exchange, and destroy. Some ancestors married off family members to the idols they worshiped as a sign of showing allegiance and commitment and continuing the cycle of serving those specific gods by the family lineage. These evil ancestral powers can marry off a man or a woman to a serpent, marine idol, or a mermaid spirit.

When born, some children are chosen and destined to take over the mantle of idol worshiping that was initially bestowed upon their ancestors and grandparents before they passed on. Suppose the destined child grows up and refuses to take up the mantle. In that case, the evil ancestral spirits begin to attack their lives, causing afflictions and infirmities and perhaps even untimely death. They do this to coerce the unwilling party to accept the responsibility. Only deliverance, rugged prayers, and the blood of Jesus can save such a person.

Evil ancestral spirits divert and cloud the destinies of people until they become unaware of who they are. They strongly and constantly monitor and survey family members' lives with what are called "watcher agents" and "familiar spirits." They continually monitor the life of the family member. They also will enter the body of such family members and even talk and give commands on their behalf. These evil powers can monitor people's lives through spiritual tattoos, physical tattoos, incisions, and even body marks.

Dealing with the Idols of our Father's House

Our ancestors worshipped many graven images and called them different names. For instance, some were called the god of thunder, the god of fruitfulness, the god of harvest, the god of sunshine, the god of rainfall, and the god of iron, etc. The truth is that these are not gods but demons worshipped by our ancestors. Our ancestors worshiped idols such as the cow, the serpent, the alligator, the goat, the crocodile, or gods affiliated with the marine kingdom. These demons were widely worshipped as gods by our ancestors, and they worshipped them by performing rituals and offering sacrifices with animals, even humans. These demons were worshipped and idolized until the dawn of Western Civilization.

Many young people are ignorant or unaware of idols in their father's house. These demonic idols may manifest in our houses through incidents such as hearing strange voices, noises, and movement of things on their own without human action. These demonic powers have brought damage to so many people because they do not understand their connection with their ancestors and idol worshiping in their lives. They have been faced with calamities such as poverty, untimely death, failure, disappointment, barrenness, genetic disorders, terminal illnesses, and marital delay.

Sometimes, unknown to many children of the ancestors, some of the grandparents made promissory notes to the idols declaring that following generations would serve them. Some of these children have been married off to demons without their knowledge. Evil forces are fighting every family connected in the past to idol worship. Until you deal with the idols in your father's house, you may never experience total deliverance in your life as a believer. The command of God is this:

"Thou shalt not make unto thee any graven image or any likeness of anything that is in Heaven above, or that is in the earth beneath, or that is in the water under the earth. Thou shalt not bow down thyself to them, nor serve them: for I the LORD thy God am a jealous God, visiting the iniquity of the fathers upon the children unto the third and fourth generation of them that hate me." -**Exodus 20:4-5**

In Christianity, an idol is anything that takes priority before God in someone's life. Christians should not make or create cult objects, carved figures, or images to use in worship; there should be no veneration of such idols. A graven image is a statue or figurine made and fashioned by human hands for worship. God prohibits creating these idols because he is spirit and he cannot be worshiped as a physical image or the works of men's hands. Rather, the worship of God should be done in spirit and truth. A good illustration is one shared by Rebecca Brown in her book *Unbroken Curses:*

A husband and wife and their three children were serving the Lord with their whole hearts. They were hardworking people, and the husband was a gifted businessman. He had done very well in business until five years prior to meeting us. Suddenly, things began to go wrong. Soon, his business failed altogether. Everything he tried failed. When we met them, both the husband and wife were working, but it seemed that they could never become stabilized financially or get ahead. They had lost their home and almost all of their material assets during those five years. They had spent much time in prayer and fasting, but it was to no avail. They felt that surely a curse was on their finances, but they could not break its power no matter how they tried. After listening to their story, we agreed that there definitely was a curse of poverty on this family. The question was, where did it come from?

Finally, we were led by the Holy Spirit to ask them what cursed objects they had in their home. They searched their minds, but they could not think of anything. We advised the family to go home, prostrate themselves on the floor before the Lord, and cry out to Him in one accord, asking Him to reveal to them what unclean thing they had in their home.

The next day they came back to the meetings very excited. They told us that they had taken our advice, gone home, and together pleaded before the Lord. As they were praying, they heard a loud crash by the front door, immediately followed by another crash in the bedroom. They jumped up to see what had fallen. By the front door had been a large, beautiful figurine that had been given to them by the husband's father, who was a very wealthy man. On one of his trips through Mexico, he had come across an exquisite and expensive figurine which stood about three feet high. It had a lead-weighted base so that it could not fall over. Because of the unusual beauty of the artwork, the man purchased it and brought it home to his son. The artistic figurine of a Mexican beggar was now smashed into a thousand pieces all over the floor![4]

God has given us the power to trample on and to fight the enemy both physically and spiritually through his grace.

To be free from the powers and idols of your father's house, you need to be delivered and be born again. Deliverance entails declaring war against the enemy through prayers. In Luke 10:19, Jesus said, "Behold, I give unto you power to tread on serpents and scorpions, and over all the power of the enemy: and nothing shall by any means hurt you."

"Therefore if any man be in Christ, he is a new creature: old things are passed away; behold, all things are become new." -**2 Corinthians 5:17**

Those who have faith in Christ are credited with his righteous life and have their sins forgiven through Christ's death. Being born again

---

[4] Page 26 of Unbroken Curses by Rebbeca Brown

means you have gotten rid of your old sinful way of life and that you are now a new creature.

Luke 18:1: *"And he spoke a parable unto them to this end that men ought always to pray, and not to faint."*

For you to be able to overcome and loosen the powers, idols, and grip of your ancestral strongholds in your father's house, you need total deliverance and prayers. All is possible through prayer; God is always listening.

Symptoms of Attack by Ancestral Powers

Symptoms are the indication of the existence of an undesirable condition. A symptom can also be a sign of an occurrence or happening. Here are some of the symptoms of attack by evil ancestral powers:

- Terrible dream attacks, including seeing your dead grandfather or grandmother in the dream, being present in your grandparents' house, seeing yourself being rubbed in white native chalk or powder, seeing yourself eating and drinking with dead people, seeing servants ruling over you or riding the horse assigned to you.
- Unending problems
- Oppression and torment
- Rising and falling, that is, repeated failure
- Unexplainable constant poverty
- Demotion
- All-around failure with no breakthrough
- Evil patterns in your life
- Diverted life journey; traveling in the opposite direction from the one that has been ordained for you.
- Stubborn blockages and embargoes
- Profitless hard work
- Get but then lose patterns
- Backwardness - you find yourself tied down to a spot like animals tied to a spot

- Spirit of bad luck. Recurrent unfortunate occurrences in your life that you did not anticipate
- Spirit of slavery where you pay for the benefits enjoyed by your ancestors
- Unpardonable errors and mistakes

How to Break Ancestral Powers and Attacks

- ✓ Repent from all known and unknown sins. Some of the sins in a generation are inheritable. One becomes guilty through association by being a descendant of a certain lineage.
- ✓ Surrender your life to Christ and be born again. Stand on God's teachings and avoid backsliding into sin as it gives the devil avenues to attack your life again.
- ✓ Use the blood of Jesus to break their hold and cover yourself with it. Jesus died on the cross for our sins and our salvation, so we are healed by his wounds.
- ✓ Stand on the promise of Colossians 2:14-15, *"blotting out the handwriting of ordinances that was against us, which was contrary to us, and took it out of the way, nailing it to his cross. And having spoiled principalities and powers, he made a shew of them openly, triumphing over them in it."* You should stand on that word and break every evil covenant in your life.
- ✓ Stand on the promise of Galatians 3:13-14, *"Christ hath redeemed us from the curse of the law, being made a curse for us: for it is written, Cursed is every one that hangeth on a tree. That the blessing of Abraham might come on the Gentiles through Jesus Christ; that we might receive the promise of the Spirit through faith."* You should stand on that word and break every curse that came about from ancestral powers and evil covenants.

Think about this:

Your forefathers who made covenants with your ancestors and idols in your family believed they did you a favor. Their notion for taking this step was to see you prosper and progress on all sides. Meanwhile, what you experience now is the direct opposite of their actions. Would you rather wail in the corner of your room or swing into action? The only action that can hasten your deliverance is prayer. It will break these traditional yokes once and for all. Remember the Bible says, *"The effective prayers of the righteous works wonders."*

You must pray without ceasing, focusing on deliverance, restoration, and eternal recovery of all that ancestral powers have stolen and destroyed in your life. Every day and night, barricade your life with the blood of Jesus and the fire of the living God so that they cannot reinforce against you.

Joel 2:25 declares: *And I will restore to you the years that the locust hath eaten, the cankerworm, and the caterpillar, and the palmerworm, my great army which I sent among you.*

Prayer Points for Deliverance from Evil Ancestral Attacks

1. I close every door of attack against my life by the blood of Jesus.
2. By the power in the blood of Jesus, I release myself from all problems originating from my ancestral line, in the name of Jesus.
3. Every ancestral and spiritual spouse troubling my marriage and stealing from me, your time is up, perish by Holy Ghost fire.
4. By the power in the blood of Jesus, I separate myself from the familiar spirit of my father's house.
5. Evil ancestral pits of my father's and mother's house, vomit my virtues and potentials in the name of Jesus.
6. I announce freedom for me from every attack launched on my life since I was an infant by Holy Ghost fire.
7. I pray that every ancestral yoke I am bound with loosens its grip on me right now.
8. My life and destiny enjoy peace from ancestral idols and serpents troubling my destiny in Jesus' name.
9. I break all foundational attack in my life by the power in the blood of Jesus.

10. I escape from the spiritual bondage holding me down from progressing in life.
11. Blood of Jesus, flush out of my blood any Satanic injections and deposits in the name of Jesus Christ.
12. My body is free from every poison deposited in my body through meals I have taken in a dream.
13. I regain the fortunes I have lost in my mother's belly in Jesus's name.
14. I also regain all I have lost from my childhood till now.
15. Blood of Jesus, deliver me from every power determined to destroy me because of my ancestors' wickedness and mistakes.
16. I recover in multifold every blessing stolen from me by ancestral powers.

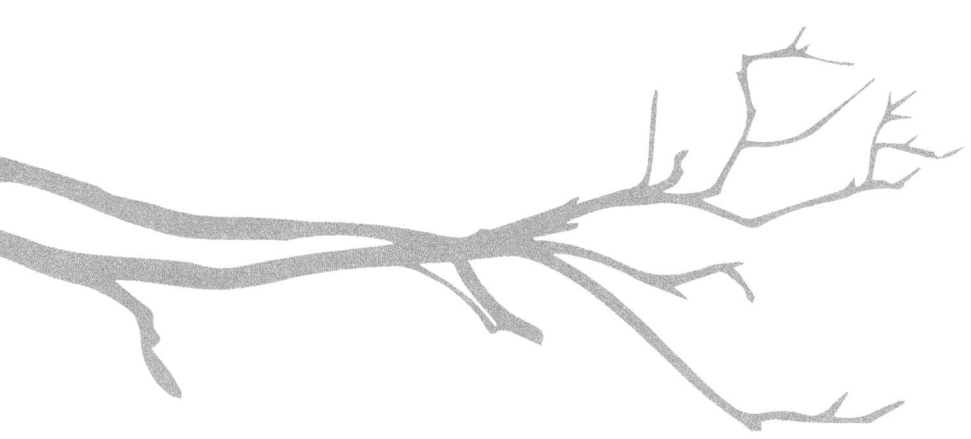

CHAPTER FIVE

How to be Free from Bitterness

> *"See to it that no one falls short of the grace of God and that no bitter root grows up to cause trouble and defile many.."*
> **Hebrews 12:15 (NIV)**

According to National Geographic, in 2004 scientists discovered what they believed to be the world's oldest living tree—a Norway spruce, the traditional "Christmas Tree" of Europe. It was found on a mountain in Sweden, and above ground it didn't look like much—only 13 feet tall. The secret to its longevity is its *root system*, which scientists estimated had been growing for about 9,550 years! (James Owen, "Oldest Living Tree Found in Sweden," news.nationalgeographic.com, 4-14-08)

The *root* of a tree is the source and sustenance of its survival; an uprooted tree or shrub will quickly dry up and die. Everything in life has a root, including bitterness. Until you trace bitterness of spirit back to its root, that is, to its cause, it will be difficult to deal with the surface issues that have resulted from it.

The Cambridge English dictionary defines bitterness as "a feeling of anger and unhappiness." Bitterness stems from hurt, harbored in one's heart, deliberately or inadvertently. Perhaps you've been betrayed by a trusted friend, or a close relation has disappointed you, and it seemed difficult to forgive them. On the other hand, maybe you've imagined or exaggerated wrongs perpetrated against you, because you feel something must be wrong somewhere. By so doing, acrimony begins to form its root in the soil of your heart.

Sadly, when bitterness starts to spread its tentacles in your heart, it doesn't just end there, it overwhelms your thoughts, and doesn't just influence your mental life, it stretches to the physical, emotional, and even your spiritual life. If you have ever been embittered, you'll agree that it can be a heavy yoke. It starts with stress, and leads to heartaches, to ill health, and to deteriorating and severed relationships with family and friends. Things you enjoyed doing before start to appear irritating, and much that you used to take for granted doesn't make sense anymore. Before you realize what is happening, you're drifting away from God and, consequently, grieving the Holy Spirit.

There's a story of a woman who complained of chronic aches and pains. Because of how overwhelming the situation was, she walked as though she carried the weight of the world on her shoulders. As a result, she looked way older than her actual age.

One day, she met a counselor who questioned her to understand why she behaved the way she did. When she was asked if she'd ever experienced any disappointments or difficulties in her life, she perked up, and her eagerness to respond was evident.

She began, "My brother robbed me of my portion of our family inheritance. Because of what he did, I didn't go to college. And don't ask me to forgive him! I never will! Just thinking about him makes me ache all over."

It was apparent that she had been bitter a long time, and because she wasn't ready to forgive and let go, the effects became obvious in her body, mind, and spirit.

An article from Johns Hopkin's Hospital states that whether it's a simple spat with your spouse or long-held resentment toward a family member or friend, unresolved conflict can go deeper than you may realize. Karen Swartz, M.D., Director of the Mood Disorders Adult Consultation Clinic at the same hospital, says that "there is an enormous physical burden to being hurt and disappointed." She further mentions that "chronic anger puts you in a fight-or-flight mode, which results in numerous changes in the heart rate, blood pressure, and immune response. And these changes increase the risk of depression, heart disease, and diabetes."

The truth is, bitterness is tolerated by many people because they are not aware of the harmful side effects. So, you may find yourself saying things like, "I'll never forget what they did." "They don't deserve another chance." Or probably asking, "God, why are you doing this to me?" Before you know it, the circumstances you face begin to define your attitude.

But God warns us about the effects of resentment in the scripture placed at the head of this chapter. The word of God reveals that if we become bound up in anger, sadness, and malice toward others, we are deficient of the grace of God. Furthermore, resentment results in many predicaments that drag us through the mud. Also, the Bible mentions that bitterness leads to rebelliousness, confusion, and all sorts of evil practices. Did you know that the attitudes of a rancorous individual can affect and infect others? Yes! Because animosity creates self-centered, self-indulgent, and irresponsible behavior. And because all you care about is centered on yourself, you begin to emit negative energy, and those around you contact it and reel in the vibe.

Now the question is, do you want to see yourself as "prey," with all the implications of helplessness rooted in that label? How long do you want to run around aimlessly in circles of hate, anger, and unnecessary jealousy? The truth is, you cannot deal with bitterness if you don't come to terms with the reality that you're suffering from it. Until you realize that you've got a stack of hurt and unforgiveness settled in your heart, you may continue to wallow in self-destruction. To deal with the venom—to excavate its root—you must take deliberate action.

Spot the Bug

Think about a computer virus. It permeates the computer and its programs, just as flu infiltrates the body's immune system and multiplies. Viruses don't spread rapidly, yet if you don't identify them at the early stage and get rid of them, you're likely to lose important files and information.

The same thing goes for bitterness. It starts small—with maybe just a wrongdoing that burrows its way into your heart. Then, consciously or unconsciously, it replays in the mind, establishing its roots in the heart. Hey! It's okay to be angry over something. It's okay to feel sad about disappointments from family and friends. You're right if you scold someone for misbehaving. But, *"'In your anger do not sin': Do not let the sun go down while you are still angry"* (Ephesians 4:26, NIV).

Many people rather prefer to bottle up their emotions, and mask their real identity. Sadly, that's not a healthy state. Emotions shouldn't be pushed down; they should be expressed. Think about this. If you put a lid on a steaming pot, the contents will eventually overrun the top and spill over. That's just how human emotions are. The more you suppress your feelings, the more you are bound to explode, even more aggressively than before.

In truth, pretending that *everything is fine*, and trying to wave our feelings away will lead to deeper resentments. Because emotions will stay suppressed till they cannot be physically kept in check anymore, then they hurt.

Sometimes we become stuck in the bitterness trench and find it difficult to climb out. However, while you cannot change what caused your bitterness, you can take deliberate actions to progress in your life and away from bitterness. And, to sever connections from the venom, you must first recognize that something is out of whack, that you feel hurt. By so doing, you have acknowledged that something is wrong and you need help. The Bible says, *"If we acknowledge our sins, he is faithful and righteous to cleanse us from all unrighteousness"* (1 John 1:9).

Rebecca Linder Hintz[5] tells of a young woman named Sally whose life was wrapped around rejection and bitterness, yet she pulled through because she recognized and admitted that there was a problem and didn't push it aside. Sally grew up in an environment that was emotionally disconnected. Although her parents weren't divorced, they insulted each other in silence and hardly ever showed love or regard. Yet, on the

---

[5] 5 steps to break free of destructive patterns by Rebecca Linder Hintz:

surface, they presented the picture of a stable, happy, and *good family*. However, her parents subtly sent hurtful messages to their children, which wounded their self-worth.

The grown-ups encouraged the kids to put up a good front to others so that they—the adults—would look good, yet the entire family was deficient in self-love. Actually, throughout Sally's childhood, her emotions weren't acknowledged or validated.

She had a low-self-esteem in junior high because she felt ugly and disliked. Nonetheless, by high school, she began to get approval from older boys by exhibiting a suggestive appearance. She was only confident when a guy looked in her direction and paid attention to her.

At 17, she got pregnant because she had the notion that if she got married and moved out of the house, she'd be free from the home environment that had left her feeling insignificant; and she thought that she'd be able to get the affection she desired by having a child. Subsequently, she got married to her baby's father, Ed. And in a pretty short time, they had six children. Unfortunately, the marriage didn't go well. It had many problems from its foundation, and in due course she got a divorce.

Years later, after her second and third marriage, an affair with a married man, and several sexually-based and futile relationships, she decided that it was time to take a deeper look within. She'd spent her entire life feeling as though something was missing, and she was done living a life that felt out of control. She eventually realized that her ex-husband Ed and the others had treated her the same way her parents did. In fact, all three of her husbands were emotionally disconnected and unwilling to accept responsibility for their issues—all of which she'd experienced as a child. Although Sally had blamed these men, she began to realize that the beliefs behind her pattern of divorce and abuse originated within her.

As time went on, Sally realized that even though she wanted to be married, she neither trusted anyone enough to connect honestly in a relationship nor believed that she was worthy of receiving a loving partner. She felt independent and stopped relying on people for help. Then, she slowly slipped into bitterness and depression. It was also discovered that at seven, she was sexually molested by an uncle. At that time, she'd tried to tell her mother about the incident, but her mom was too busy to listen, so she decided not to say anything for many years.

When she finally told her family, her father didn't want to acknowledge what had happened because he didn't want to make waves. Once again, it was more important to look good than to publicly divulge this embarrassing family secret.

Now, because of Sally's abuse, she made some vital decisions in her life and was bent on keeping to them. She concluded that:

1. She'd not rely on anyone—not even God—to help her.

2. Something was wrong with her; otherwise, the abuse wouldn't have happened.

3. She had no control over her life (which led to the development of a victim mentality).

4. She was inadequate and didn't deserve good things.

Regrettably, these weren't all that happened to her. The ideas she embraced perpetuated a good number of bad behaviors like a proclivity for eating disorders, infidelity, a need to rebel against authority, and misuse of her sexual energy. She stored resentment and blame because she felt betrayed, yet her ultimate betrayal was of herself. She hated herself and had a one-sided self-image. She'd inherited not only her parents' low self-worth but also the desire to repress deep fears of unworthiness and mask them with an external world that looked good.

But because she had to move forward, she acknowledged that things were getting out of hand, and sought help. She didn't justify her actions and bitterness; she spotted the venom, spoke up, and decided to turn over a new leaf, for the betterment of her life. Although she took some time to heal completely, she could love herself again.

Lysa Tekurst also shared how God delivered her from suppressed anger that turned to bitterness after her friend hurt her feelings. She emphasized how she was bent out of shape. And everyone in the house knew she wasn't happy. She tried all she could to regain a state of calm and gentleness in her life, tone, and temper, but it was futile. She said, "I quoted verses. I rebuked Satan. I bossed my feelings around with Truth; I even tried to take a nap. But none of these activities soothed me."

What finally got to her was a smell that slowly filled her room, a stench strong-scented candles couldn't mask. And, unfortunately, she couldn't figure out what it was or where it came from, and the mysterious, awful smell continued to waft through her home.

Then she discovered that one of her daughters had placed a kitchen trash can in the corner of her bedroom to toss scraps of paper in it as she worked on a school project. At the bottom of that trash can had been placed some old food in the final stages of rot. She said, "I didn't have the heart to find out what the rot was; I just knew the trash can had to go. Immediately."

The smell was an external indication of an internal situation. And the trash can wasn't the only thing that stunk that night, she realized; so did her attitude. And that inner bitterness was causing a "stench" in her life, just like the rotten food at the bottom of the trash can had been stinking up the house—until it was thrown out.

She said, "The reason I couldn't be soothed by quoting Scripture, bossing my feelings, rebuking Satan, or even taking a nap is that God wanted me to be aware of my stink—something inside of me that stunk—a place starting to rot."

The reality of the matter is, she'd been hurt by someone she trusted and wasn't ready to confront the issue or forgive the person who hurt her. Rather, she stuffed bitterness in her heart and tried to pretend it wasn't there. But the rot was there, and the stink from deep within her heart kept spilling out in her attitudes and actions.

She understood that God didn't want her to temporarily mask the situation by suppressing her feelings. Rather, he wanted her to address the root of the rot—to see it, admit it, expose it and let him clean it up. Immediately.

What's in Your Heart?

"Keep thy heart with all diligence; for out of it are the issues of life." **-Proverbs 4:23**

It's not enough to identify and admit that there's a problem. You must be ready to deal with yourself and also be deliberate about what is contained in your heart. One thing about roots is that they grow deep down, beneath the exterior, where the eyes cannot see. They are firmly grounded so that they become established before sprouting up and producing fruit—which everyone sees. It is the same with bitterness. So, there's more to do than just spotting the bug!

The heart is the seat of thoughts, will, and emotions. Anything that goes on in the heart is reflected on the outside. The Bible rightly says, *"For as [a man] thinketh in his heart, so is he"* (Proverbs 23:7). Your thoughts indeed define you because you cannot act contrary to what you think. When bitterness is seated in your heart, it will definitely affect everyone with whom you come in contact, and go on to make you question your faith.

The Word of God reveals in the Book of Ruth a typical example of a woman who was bitter in the heart so much that she blamed God for her resentments. Her name was Naomi—a name which means, ironically, pleasant—and she was the wife of Elimelech. Elimelech went with his wife and two sons from Bethlehem to the country of Moab as there was a food shortage in the land. While in Moab, the sons found two women—Ruth and Orpah, who were among the native people—and married them. But unfortunately, Elimelech and his two sons died in Moab and left Naomi, Ruth, and Orpah to care for themselves.

When Naomi heard that the famine in the land of Judah had lifted, she made up her mind to return home to her relatives. But when she wanted to leave, Orpah and Ruth followed her. Along the way, Naomi presented the women with the option of retiring to their hometown, yet they refused. They told her, *"We want to go with you to your people."* But Naomi said:

"Why should you go on with me? Can I still give birth to other sons who could grow up to be your husbands? No, my daughters, return to your parents' homes, for I am too old to marry again. And even if it were possible, and I were to get married tonight and bear sons, then what? Would you wait for them to grow up and refuse to marry someone else? No, of course not, my daughters! **Things are far more bitter for me than for you because the LORD himself has caused me to suffer**" (Ruth 1:10-14, NLT, emphasis added).

Orpah turned back, but Ruth was resolute to both Naomi and her God. So only Naomi and Ruth continued on their journey. When they came to Bethlehem, the whole municipality was stimulated by their appearance. The women wondered if it was Naomi:

"Is it really Naomi?" the women asked.

"Don't call me Naomi," she responded. "Instead, call me Mara [which means bitter], *for the Almighty has made life very bitter for me. I went away full, but the Lord has brought me home empty. Why call me Naomi when the Lord has caused me to suffer and the Almighty has sent such tragedy upon me?"* **-Ruth 1:19-21 (NLT)**

Do you wonder what would have caused the whole town to stir? Could it have been Naomi's look? Or, maybe they saw on her face the changes that took place in her heart. Pay attention to what she says in verses 19-21—Naomi's heart was already drowned in bitterness, and she'd concluded that it was God who caused her to be bitter.

Perhaps you're going through such a difficult situation as this, or maybe worse; you must purge your heart of every lie that God is inflicting pain on you. Understand that God cares for and desires the best for you. The fact is, he's not ignorant of our struggles, yet he wants us to acknowledge that it's out of our hands, and run to him for help.

God doesn't want his children to succumb to the devices of the enemy and wallow in bitterness of heart. That's why he says, *"But be not conformed to this world: but be ye transformed by the renewing of your mind, that ye may prove what is that good and acceptable, and the perfect will of God."* **-Romans 12:2**

How then do you renew your mind?

House the word in your Heart

You can only transform your mind through the Word of God. The only counter weapon against the enemy of bitterness is the Word of God. When you study the Word and understand that God's plans for you are of peace—to give you hope and a joyous outcome—you will operate in a different dimension, above anger and hurt.

The psalmist understood the importance of possessing God's Word in the heart. That's why he wrote, *"Thy word have I hid in my heart that I might not sin against you."* **-Psalm 119:11**

Like I earlier mentioned, bitterness doesn't just affect one aspect of your life. It eats you up from the mental to the physical to the spiritual side of your life. Indeed, bitterness is a sin, because God hates unforgiveness and warns against jealousy, malice and bearing grudges. The Bible says bitterness disconnects us from the grace of God, and that's a warning to believers.

Nonetheless, if you take in the Word of God daily, when you're faced with problems, you'll discover you'll be dishing out words of comfort and promises concerning your life, and you'll be too filled with the Word to leave room for hate and anger to settle.

Stand on Bended Knees

Have you ever been so weighed down with a burden that, when you got to your prayer closet, all you did was scream, roll on the floor, cry, and pour out your heart without holding back? How did you feel when you come out of the prayer room? You felt relieved, didn't you? Yes, we all do!

God loves to commune with his children. He loves to listen to our cries and heartaches. And remember that prayer is a two-way thing. As you speak to him, he listens, then responds, and we listen. Everyone likes to have that one friend who hears them out when they vent. That one person they can always run to when they hit rock bottom—so they can just share their hearts, heave a sigh and feel okay. Can you relate? I'm sure you can!

If our earthly friends can give us solace and make the load seem lighter, why not try Jesus? A popular church hymn says,

> *"What a friend we have in Jesus,*
> *All our sins and grieves to bear*
> *What a privilege to carry*
> *Everything to God in prayer.*
> ***Oh, what peace we often forfeit;***
> ***Oh, what needless pain we bear***
> ***All because we do not carry everything to God in prayer.***

Isn't it beautiful how God has granted us access to himself, through Jesus? Isn't it amazing that you can always call on the name of the Lord, whenever you want and wherever you are? What then is hindering you from calling on the Father for help?

God is reaching out to you right now. He says, *"Do not be anxious about anything, but in every situation, by prayer and petition, with thanksgiving, present your requests to God"* (Philippians 4:6, NIV). He has also promised that whenever you call upon him—especially in times of trouble—he will answer you. Isn't bitterness trouble enough? Isn't it life-threatening enough? Why then haven't you gone on bended knees?

Learn from Hannah, the barren woman in 1 Samuel. How hard it must have been for her as a wife without a child in the culture of that day. Imagine the ridicule from her co-wife and other women in the community. Yet, as much as she cried and felt terrible, she didn't allow the situation to shade her hope in God.

Was she overwhelmed by her situation? Absolutely! Just like any barren woman, she was overcome by her emotions. Here's the proof:

"Her husband said, 'Oh Hannah, why are you crying? Why aren't you eating? And why are you so upset? Am I not more worth to you than ten sons?" **-1 Samuel 1:8 (MSG)**

But guess what? Rather than just sit and cry, lament and lose trust, she went to God in prayer!

"So Hannah…pulled herself together, slipped away quietly, and entered the sanctuary. The priest Eli was on duty at the entrance to God's Temple in the customary seat. **Crushed in soul, Hannah prayed to God** *and cried and cried—inconsolably. Then she made a vow:*

> *Oh, God-of-the-Angel-Armies,*
> *If you'll take a good, hard look at my pain,*
> *If you'll quit neglecting me and go into action for me*
> *By giving me a son,*
> *I'll give him completely, unreservedly to you.*
> *I'll set him apart for a life of holy discipline.* **-1 Samuel 1:9-11 (MSG)**

How does it feel to know that someone has been through heartache, yet refused to give in to bitterness? The Bible says that even as Hannah was praying, the priest accused her of being drunk with wine. But she told him she was a woman of sorrow and wasn't drunk, instead, she was seeking the Lord. And guess what? God answered her request—and her bitterness was uprooted!

Let It Go!

"To forgive is to set a prisoner free and discover that the prisoner was you. - Lewis B. Smedes

The matter of forgiveness goes beyond a mere narrow religious theme. Rather, it's a matter vital to our very life. Everyone has been hurt by either the actions or words of another. Perhaps as a child, your parents used to criticize you. As an adult, maybe your partner had an affair with someone else. Or you may have had a traumatizing experience— emotional or physical abuse by either a family member or someone else you trusted. Such wounds can indeed leave you with a lasting feeling of acrimony, and sometimes you may want to go as far as turning the tables on them.

This is where the rubber meets the road. As much as forgiveness is for the offender, the offended benefits more from the act. How? When you choose to let it go, you free yourself from the grip of bitterness and enjoy improved health and peace of mind. On the other hand, if you dwell on your wounds and hurts, bitterness can take root, and leave you bound. Yes, forgiveness maybe difficult, yet it is relieving and freeing.

God First Forgave You

So, what is forgiveness? The Merriam Webster dictionary defines the term as: "to cease to feel resentment against (an offender): pardon." Irrespective of how challenging it may seem to pardon someone who hurt you deeply, God commands us to forgive people, just as he forgave us our sins. He says, *"Bear with each other and forgive one another if any of you has a grievance against someone. Forgive as the Lord forgave you."* -**Colossians 3:13 (NIV)**

God showed us mercy through Jesus when he came to die for our sins. This implies that we have been forgiven by the blood of the lamb—there was an exchange of life, at the cross, and we must extend this act of forgiveness to others and show grace to them as well.

Here is an example of what I mean when I say that Jesus exchanged his life for ours. In a World War I trench, a soldier was dying. This soldier had a friend who had lived a lawless life before the war, spent time in prison, made many bad choices, and even at that moment was still sought by the police. The dying man called his friend to him, drew his face down near his, and then removed his own dog tag—that his, his ID—and shoved it into the friend's hand. He said, "Listen, you've had a ruthless life. The police are on the lookout for you, but I don't have any convictions against me. My record is spotless, so take my dog tag, my documents, my good name, and consider them your own. And give me your dog tag and papers, and I'll die with them in your name—take your crimes with me into the grave. Give you a new start in life."

This is exactly what Jesus did for us—took our sin with him to the cross so that we could have a new start in life. Remember that he wasn't guilty of any wrongdoings, yet he suffered in our stead—took the beatings and shame that we should have borne—and forgave us and set us free from our iniquities. Oh, what a heart!

Now It's Your Turn!

You cannot claim to be a believer if you can't forgive. The story is told of Elisabeth Eliot, whose husband Jim Eliot was a missionary to a South American Indian tribe. Jim Eliot was eventually murdered by this same tribe that he had devoted his life to help. Elisabeth remarried after some years, and her second husband died of cancer. After her second husband's death, she remained a widow. Although she was heartbroken by the murder of her first husband, she still went back to preach to the Indians—the same tribe that executed her husband.

Let's pause here and ponder! This is such a brave act by this dear Christian woman! How easy it would have been for her to instead pray for those who had killed her husband to be killed themselves. How easy to seek her own revenge. But no! She had to dig up the root of bitterness against those who hurt her by reaching out to them with the Gospel of

Christ. Amazingly, she became free of the animosity she had for these Indians. You cannot deal with bitterness if you can't forgive. Forgiveness digs up the root of what triggered the rage and sting in your heart and gives your mind rest.

There's a character in the Bible whose story of forgiveness is phenomenal. His name is Joseph! The story of Joseph and his brothers in Genesis 37 is tragic, but rich in life lessons. The Bible points out that Joseph was the most loved of his father. Consequently, his brothers got jealous of him, and his gifts. Then, when he reached the age of seventeen, his brothers decided to take action against him. At first, they wanted to kill him. But they sold him off to a passing slave-trader.

"And they said one to another, 'Behold this dreamer cometh. Come now, therefore, and let us slay him and cast him into some pit, and we will say some evil beast hath devoured him: and we shall see what shall become of his dreams…Then there passed by Midianite merchantmen, and they drew and lifted up Joseph out of the pit, and sold Joseph to the Ishmeelites for twenty pieces of silver: and they brought Joseph into Egypt." **-Genesis 37:19-20, 28**

It didn't end there; subsequently, they reported his death to their father. Hey! Let's take a halt here! Can you put yourself in Joseph's shoes? Can you feel the tears that welled up in his eyes as he felt betrayed by his siblings? How about the fact that he'll not see his father and younger brother again? Can you find anger, hatred, and bitterness taking their roots in his heart? Imagine him saying silently in his heart, "Why me Lord? Where did I go wrong?"

One of the most painful betrayals is that of family. Family is where you should feel safe, and secure. But when they turn their back on you, or outright reject you like they did Joseph, and you don't have anyone to look up to, it can lead to depression at its deepest, bitterness in its worst form, and render you hopeless and helpless. This was Joseph's plight.

However, something astounding happened! A time came when Joseph's brothers had to go to where Joseph was at the time, and Joseph was the Governor of Egypt! There was a severe famine where his brothers were, and they had to go down to Egypt in search of grain—which meant they would have to pass through their brother to get the grain.

What would you do if you were joseph? Arrest them? Take them as slaves? Return them? Or kill them? These thoughts may have run through Joseph's mind. But guess what he did? He didn't allow his bitter past to influence his actions. He put aside his grievances against his brothers and helped them. He may have struggled with his feelings toward his brothers. But he forgave them; he moved past resentment and bitterness and sullenness.

"Then Joseph could not refrain himself before all them that stood by him; and he cried, Cause every man to go out from me. And there stood no man with him, while Joseph made himself known unto his brothers. And he wept aloud; the Egyptians and the house of Pharaoh heard. And Joseph said unto his brethren, I am Joseph; doth my father yet live? And his brethren could not answer him for they were troubled at his presence... Now therefore, be not grieved, nor angry with yourselves, that ye sold me hither: for God did send me before you to preserve life." -**Genesis 45:1-3, 5**

Joseph had every reason to torture his brothers. Yet he refused to, and chose forgiveness. Perhaps your situation is like Joseph's. You need to ask God for the grace to forgive and let go to rise above the waves of bitterness. Forgiveness purifies the heart of hurt and discomfort and digs out the root of bitterness as well. Also, when you release annoyance, hatred, and hostility, you begin to feel sympathy, kind-heartedness and at times even love for the person who offended you. Can you relate? Get ready to forgive that person you've held a grudge for all this time. If Joseph could, you too can!

Stay Allied to Sweetness

The ultimate way of dealing with the root of bitterness is having an intimate relationship with God. Intimate here connotes connectedness—so much that the life of Christ flows through you, without any interferences. Remember that bitterness establishes its root when there is a problem that hasn't been surrendered to Jesus.

Scripture reveals that those who trust in the Lord receive help from Him. It says, *"The righteous cry out, and the Lord hears them; he delivers them from all their troubles. The Lord is close to the brokenhearted and* saves those who are crushed in spirit. The righteous person may have many troubles, but the Lord delivers him from them all." -**Psalm 34:17-19**

This means that just because you're a believer, God is out to deliver you from your troubles, and give you rest. If you want to build a deeper and closer relationship with him, then be sure to put him first in every situation you may find yourself in.

The truth is, God has made his grace available to provide all we need, for each situation we may encounter. From strength to wisdom to discernment, he has given us all we need to respond in Christ, rather than self, when life throws ugly events at us.

God never offered a smooth journey, without hitches along the road. But he's promised that help will always come in time. Sometimes pain swamps us, and it seems impossible that someday we will cease to hurt and our hearts will be whole again. Nonetheless, when your life is yielded to God, you can always trust to live above bitterness, and your heart will thrive again.

Kelly R. Baker[6] shares her story of how God healed her of bitterness because she had a personal relationship with him. According to her, growing up, she lived in constant terror of her father, because he used to suppress them with destructive and battering words and behavior. She said she learned early to subdue her actual emotional state, point of view, and ideas to survive. She longed for when she'd become grown up enough to leave the house—her parents—and eventually break free.

Thank goodness, the time came. But it was quite unfortunate that she wasn't really free yet. The deep wound that her father inflicted on her formed a bitter root and kept poisoning her life with tainted fruit. She clung to angry, hateful, and painful feelings towards her father. This also affected her relationship with other men, because she could neither trust nor respect men. Her identity was crippled by believing many of the things her father said to her, which made her struggle with suicidal thoughts.

However, there is good news! She met God! In her words: "In my most desperate time, God found me. I gave my life to Jesus when I was 17 years old. The truth that I have a heavenly Father who loves

---

[6] Kelly R. Baker: *This, Made Me FREE from Bitterness and Resentment*,

me unconditionally and who will never abuse me and control me, but instead support and encourage me till the end, was a fountain of life to me. It pulled me back from the edge of the pit I was about to throw myself in and gave me meaning and a reason to live. But this was just the beginning."

That was when the journey to her healing began. She mentioned that after many years—by this time, she had gotten married, and moved to a different country—the Holy Spirit took her gradually but firmly on a journey of freedom from bitterness and hatred. She said, "We started with the relationship with my father. The more I spent time every day in prayer and God's Word, the clearer the path to healing became." God's Word and prayer are the only means through which the Father can be accessed and where we can find his promises for our lives.

She said, "The first step was forgiveness. For the first time, I realized that forgiveness is a process. I need to stay in forgiveness and choose forgiveness whenever resentful thoughts and feelings enter my mind." Then she talked about how that forgiveness is tangible. She stated that she was often led back in her memories to write down the precise ways her father hurt her. Because God's grace was sufficient, she could open the painful doors again, and close them forever, while acknowledging the hurt and pain.

Although she had released her father from his dues, she still felt the hurt sometimes—they lingered. And she said, "God was inviting me to grieve and mourn the losses I have experienced. With the help of the Psalms I could lament and find words to express not only painful and conflicting feelings, but also hope and trust in God as the Judge, Redeemer, and Vindicator of my suffering."

As time went on, she declared that she began to see her father as a person who is a captive—in pain. Then her heart became softened toward him. Amazingly, that was God, healing her emotions. She confessed that God's love could now flow freely in her heart and find its way out in her communication with her father. Even though it was still difficult for her to maintain a relationship with him, the barrier of resentment from her side was gone.

This is what having a relationship with God can do! God alone can pull us out of the dungeon of dismay and erase every bitterness from our hearts. Like I mentioned earlier, it's okay to go through the rough path of life; it's okay to struggle to forgive and keep a straight attitude toward people. It's not out of place to cry and decide to shut the world out of your life. But after all these, know that God loves you. He's the only source of happiness, sweetness, contentment, and peace of mind.

At the end of yourself, you are just empty and dry. You must recognize that you can't do it all by yourself. The Word of God says that it's only the Spirit of God that can help us in our times of weakness. Now the question is, what happens if you don't know Jesus? An old cliché says, NO JESUS, NO PEACE. KNOW JESUS, KNOW PEACE. Which side do you belong to? Seek Jesus now, and experience eternal sweetness in your life.

Have a Support System

A friend loves at all times, and a brother is born for a time of adversity. **-Proverbs 17:17 (NIV)**

Bitterness feeds on isolation! Yet through talking to someone—a close friend, family member, or therapist—you can explore the help the issue that caused the hurt which escalated to bitterness. Resentments, if neglected, can overpower you and even become toxic to you.

The truth is that bitterness can be quite the battle to move on from. And sometimes the strongest tactic and easiest way forward is to open up to someone—or to a group of people—and accept help. Perhaps you have a friend who listens patiently and doesn't judge, then that's perfect! However, if you need an unbiased viewpoint and a safe place to confide in someone outside your circle, you can try a support group, a counselor, or a psychologist. They will offer professional help and assist you out of the situation.

The Apostle Paul understood the need for having a support system, which is why he encouraged the believers in Colossians 3:13 to bear one another's burden. Learn to talk to someone about how you feel and be open-minded so you can receive help.

"make sure there is no root among you that produces such bitter poison." **-Deuteronomy 29:18b**

A person whose heart has been gripped with the root of bitterness is always angry, irrespective of how they try to control it. Like a toxic wild plant, the only sure solution is to deal with the issue from its root. However, you can soar above the wiles of the enemy, and overcome bitterness. But it will require deliberateness and an act of will. Sometimes, it's risky, yet you have to choose to let go and be freed.

Maybe you are still holding onto the past, reliving its hurts over and over again in your mind and emotions; thus, you struggle with bitterness. It's time to choose to uproot that poisonous plant. How do you achieve this? You will need to return to the incident in your memory, and allow God to renew your mind. Consciously seek his help to guide you in the process, so you can release yourself from a sense of responsibility for bringing about justice, and you can release others as well.

Digging up bitterness from its root creates a sweet and amazing atmosphere for your life. When the origin of hurt and pain is dealt with, the root withers and dies. Then you'll realize that the ugly feeling goes with it as well, leaving room for the fruit of the Spirit to spring forth. But remember that you must submit to God, and allow him to guide you through the process of healing because he alone can dig up the root of bitterness from your life.

Prayer Points

1. Heavenly Father, I thank you for your grace upon my life. Thank you for your Word that assures me that when I look up to you, I'm enlightened, and my face is not ashamed. And that you will always hear me when I cry out to you.
2. I come to you with a heavy heart—of bitterness—and I ask that you heal me, and make me whole again. Flush out everything that wasn't planted by you, and set me free from this pain and sullenness.
3. Every evil dropped into my life, destiny, and career, Lord, let your blood wash it out of my system.
4. Every strange thing in my body, Lord, search my life, bring all the strange things out, and destroy them all.

5. We are thankful to you for being our shield, for being our protection, and for being our safety, not only for us but for our loved ones as well, in Jesus's name.
6. Oh Lord! I thank you for the free oxygen to breathe and the ability to wake up on this glorious day.
7. I set myself free from every curse attached to any evil covenant that came as a result of bitterness and an unforgiving spirit, in the name of Jesus.
8. I come against every repercussion of breaking unconscious covenants—be washed away by the blood of the Lamb!
9. Thank you, Lord, because I know that you have heard and answered my prayers, in Jesus' name, amen.

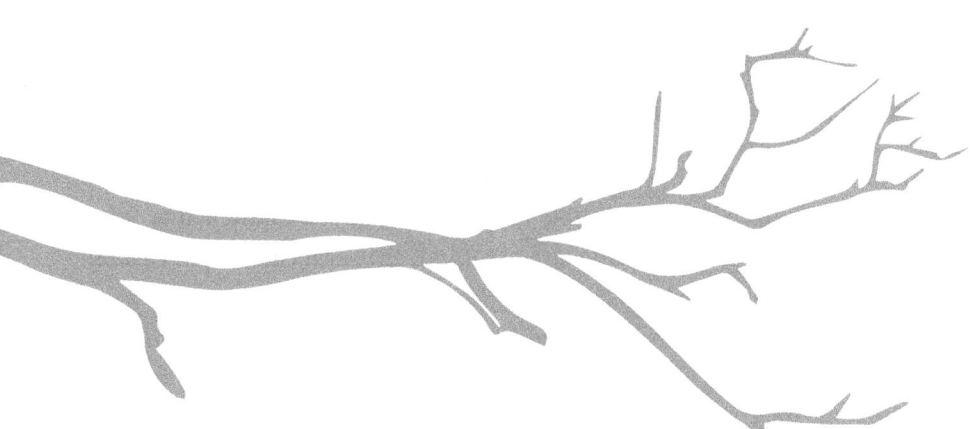

CHAPTER SIX

Breaking the Evil Ancestral Grip on Your Destiny

The "Tsar Bomba"—Russian for "King of Bombs—is the most powerful weapon ever detonated. A thermonuclear bomb, it was detonated in a nuclear weapons test by the Soviet Union over an island in the Arctic Ocean on October 30, 1961. The explosion was almost 4,000 times more powerful than that of the U. S. bomb that wiped out Hiroshima in World War II. According to the Encyclopedia Britannica, it produced "a mushroom cloud more than 37 miles (60 km) high" and a detonation flash "seen some 620 miles (1,000 km) away." The blast levelled "an uninhabited village 34 miles (55 km) from ground zero" and "buildings more than 100 miles (160 km) away were reportedly damaged. In addition, it was estimated that heat from the blast would have caused third-degree burns up to 62 miles (100 km) distant." (https://www.britannica.com/topic/Tsar-Bomba)

Ancestral Weapons

Human beings have created some powerful weapons with which to destroy one another, but the Bible reveals that our spiritual enemy, Satan, has also fashioned weapons against. God, through the prophet Isaiah, referred to these weapons:

*"No **weapon** that is **formed against thee** shall prosper, and every tongue that shall rise against thee in judgment thou shalt condemn. This is the heritage of the servants of the LORD, and their righteousness is of me, saith the LORD."* -**Isaiah 54:17, emphasis added**

Evil ancestral powers have various *weapons "formed against thee"* to maintain their grip on your destiny—to hinder you from achieving your dreams, goals, and God-given purpose. Weapons are dual-purpose tools, used for both attack and defense. Evil ancestral powers use their weapons to attack you and keep you down. But, as Isaiah 54:17 says, they cannot prosper against *"the servants of the LORD"* who know their rights in Jesus.

God, and God alone, has the power and might to make the evil weapons formed against you to fail, but he won't do it until you are ready. God promises that your destiny has been kept safe in him. Now he wants to hand you the spiritual weapons necessary to defend against the attacks of the enemy to achieve your destiny. Are you ready to receive those weapons and to use them in Jesus' name?

Spiritual Weapons

God fights for you through his weapons. But as he fights for you, it is important that you also rise in authority to take charge of your life. God's Word will only come to pass in your life if you take the step of faith to bring it into reality. You must substantiate God's Word in your life by acting on it.

The Bible says: *"The weapons we fight with are not the weapons of the world. On the contrary, they have divine power to demolish strongholds"* (2 Corinthians 10:4, NIV). You see, we can only overcome ancestral weapons with spiritual weapons. Let's look now at some of the spiritual weapons God has given us, according to the Scriptures:

God's Word

"For the word of God is quick, and powerful, and sharper than any twoedged sword" -**Hebrews 4:12**

Let us learn from our dear Lord, Jesus Christ. When he was tempted by Satan in the wilderness, each time he countered the temptation with a quote from Scripture (Matthew 4:1-11). If Jesus used the Word against Satan, we should too. Profane words cannot defeat Satan, nor can our carnal or worldly wisdom, nor our self-righteousness. God's Word alone has the ultimate power over every circumstance.

Prayer

Prayer is another of the mighty spiritual weapons God has given us.

"Pray without ceasing" -**1 Thessalonians 5:17**

Everything is possible through prayer. The confidence you have in prayer is that God always hears you when you pray according to his will; and because he does, he grants your desires (1 John 5:14-15). Through prayers, your yoke will break, and you will gain your liberty.

"Be careful for nothing; but in everything by prayer and supplication with thanksgiving let your requests be made known unto God." -**Philippians 4:6**

You should pray in Jesus' name to reverse and cancel every evil done against you and your family by serpent, marine, and familiar spirits. Plead the blood of Jesus over yourself in your prayer. Rebuke every spiritual transaction formed against you to steal, kill, exchange and destroy your life.

In prayer, you have the grace to denounce spiritual transactions that have been formed through sexual intercourse, handshakes, food, drinks, money, DNA (e.g., by means of samples of your hair, nails, blood, body fluids), or through anything representing you, including your pictures or possessions.

And you should continue to *"pray without ceasing"* even after your wishes have been granted. You can either pray in the spirit or in understanding.

Fasting

"However, this kind does not go out except by prayer and fasting." -**Matthew 17:21**

Fasting is another spiritual weapon God has given us. The battle against ancestral strongholds is a spiritual activity that requires you to deny yourself some enjoyments or luxuries, particularly those that you think you would not survive without. It helps you to concentrate on what you are asking God for: your deliverance and liberty. It is a wonderful strategy for spiritual warfare. It beats all ancestral weapons, no matter how strongly they were put together.

Thanksgiving

"Give thanks in all circumstances; for this is God's will for you in Christ Jesus." -**1 Thessalonians 5:18 (NIV)**

Along life's road, you'll encounter sunshine and rain, roses and thorns. Sometimes, the going is gentle and smooth; at another time, it may be rough and bumpy. Nonetheless, no matter what comes your way, God wants you to respond to him with a heart of thanksgiving. He does not want you to grumble or complain. By so doing, you remain separate from unbelievers who are selfish and only want to ask till their needs are met. Thanksgiving is a powerful spiritual weapon.

The Armor of God

"Finally, be strong in the Lord and in his mighty power. Put on the full armor of God, so that you can take your stand against the devil's schemes. For our struggle is not against flesh and blood, but against the rulers, against the authorities, against the powers of this dark world and against the spiritual forces of evil in the heavenly realms." -**Ephesians 6:10-12**

The *"full armor of God"* is central to our weaponry. The text above tells us to *"be strong in the Lord."* Being strong here means being confident and encouraged in the Lord. That is the core step in facing and rendering powerless every ancestral weapon in your life, business, family, and so on.

Don't ignore the truth that you need confidence to set God's armor in action in every area of your life, and be sure to *"Put on the **full** armor of God,"* which is fundamental to totally defeating and gaining victory over ancestral weapons. According to Ephesians 6, the full armor of God includes the following:

> **The Belt of Truth**
> *"Then you will know the truth, and the truth will set you free."* -**John 8:32 (NIV)**
>
> Truth is one of the virtues of the spirit. The Lord wants you to walk and serve him in truth. Truth can set you free from bondage, shackles, and disturbance. He wants you to spread the truth in his Word to others. Also, he wants you to apply the truth in the Scriptures to your life and your relationship with friends, family, colleagues, acquaintances, and neighbors.

> **Breastplate of Righteousness**
> *"God made him who had no sin to be sin for us, so that in him we might become the righteousness of God."* -**2 Corinthians 5:21 (NIV)**
>
> Righteousness means right-standing with God. You need to put on righteousness like a breastplate or as closely fitting as your clothes. Righteousness guides your behavior and heart at all times, even when you find yourself surrounded with gross wickedness.

> **Gospel of Peace**
> *"…and with your feet fitted with the readiness that comes from the gospel of peace."* -**Ephesians 6:15**
> *"For I am not ashamed of this Good News about Christ. It is the power of God at work, saving everyone who believes—the Jew first and also the Gentile."* -**Romans 1:16 (NLT)**
>
> The gospel is good news. Again, good news brings peace and salvation. You need to stand unshaken in the peace that God's

Word gives. Worry, panic, anxiety, war, threat, and diseases might want to pull you away from the foundation of God's Word that you are standing on, but don't fret. Stand firm. You have the surest anchor; God's Word that brings peace.

- ➢ **Shield of Faith**

"In addition to all of these, hold up the shield of faith to stop the fiery arrows of the devil." -**Ephesians 6:16 (NLT)**

In a war, a shield is used for protection against arrows or other weapons. Now, the Lord wants you to swing your faith into action in your spiritual warfare. Faith is your shield; it keeps, protects, and guards you. Faith is not supposed to lie dormant in you. It should be exercised. The more you exercise it, the more it grows. Mind you, your faith also grows by feeding it with God's Word.

- ➢ **Helmet of Salvation**

"And take the helmet of salvation." -**Ephesians 6:17**

Warriors wear helmets for protection, as do cyclists, astronauts, and so on. The purpose is to prevent injury to the head. The head is the vital part of the body that must be heavily protected.

Remember the Bible mentioned that the mind is a battlefield. The mind is housed in the head. Therefore, the enemies will attack your mind with unholy, unfitting thoughts so that you might sin against God. Thank God for his Word. His Word will serve as a helmet to your head and mind against these attacks. God's Word will purify and save your mind.

You've been held captive and entangled in sin; only God's Word can bring you salvation. His living Word is a tool to offer liberty and freedom to you and heal your broken heart. God's salvation to you delivers you from eternal condemnation and the consequences associated with disobedience to God's commandments; that salvation is found in Jesus alone.

- ➢ **Sword of the Spirit**

"...and the sword that the Spirit wields, which is the Word of God." -**Ephesians 6:17**

"Your word is a lamp to my feet and a light to my path." -**Psalm 119:105**

"For the word of God is alive and active. Sharper than any double-edged sword, it penetrates even to dividing soul and spirit, joints and marrow; it judges the thoughts and attitudes of the heart." -**Hebrews 4:12 (NIV)**

The sword of the Spirit is the Word of God found in the Bible. Using the sword of the Spirit goes beyond swinging the Holy Book in various directions in prayer. It is the amount of God's Word that lives in your heart. This Word fights your battles, directs your path, and unshackles you.

When God's Word richly fills your heart, you are not caught unaware by the troubles and attacks of the enemy. You do not need to hold your Bible physically. The Holy Spirit will surely bring to your remembrance what you have studied and bless you with utterances of his Word.

Think about this:

The evil ancestral grip is like a captor holding people hostage. The captor controls the destiny of his hostages and determines what is going to happen to them. Yet, you can change things. Determining what goes on in your life will be your business.

Handle your life with seriousness and guard it with the spiritual armor that God provides you in His word. If you do not take action, God will not do it on your behalf. Therefore, be spiritually attuned. Get hold of your life by hanging on to God's promises for you. Enjoy the power in the name of Jesus, the Word of God, and prayer.

Prayers to Break the Evil Ancestral Grip on Your Destiny

Declare this Bible passage into your life:

"The Spirit of the Lord God *is upon me; because the* Lord *hath anointed me to preach good tidings unto the meek; he hath sent me to bind up the brokenhearted, to proclaim liberty to the captives, and the*

opening of the prison to them that are bound. To proclaim the acceptable year of the LORD, *and the day of vengeance of our God; to comfort all that mourn."* **-Isaiah 61:1-2**

Pray these prayers:

1. May all demonic gates in my life be shut, and every spirit of the enemy be bound.
2. I receive the Holy Spirit and the blessings of adoption, compassion, consideration, counsel, courage, devotion, intelligence, direction, discernment, discretion, excellence, edification, fairness, faith, faithfulness, fear of God, liberty, freedom, forgiveness, glory, goodness, grace, gratitude, harmony, healing, holiness, honesty, humility, joy, justice, kindness, knowledge, understanding, and soundness of mind, power, love, and meekness. May all these qualities overshadow me now.
3. I claim them in the mighty name of Jesus.
4. I receive abundant peace from Jesus. Jesus takes glory in my life henceforth.
5. I am released from the clutch of my ancestors.
6. I renounce the sins of my ancestors that are haunting me.
7. I receive forgiveness from the consequences of my forefathers' sins.
8. The power in the blood of Jesus washes, cleanses, and disconnects me from all ancestral ties.
9. I am free from the power of the idols in my lineage.
10. I am covered with the precious blood of Jesus. Amen!

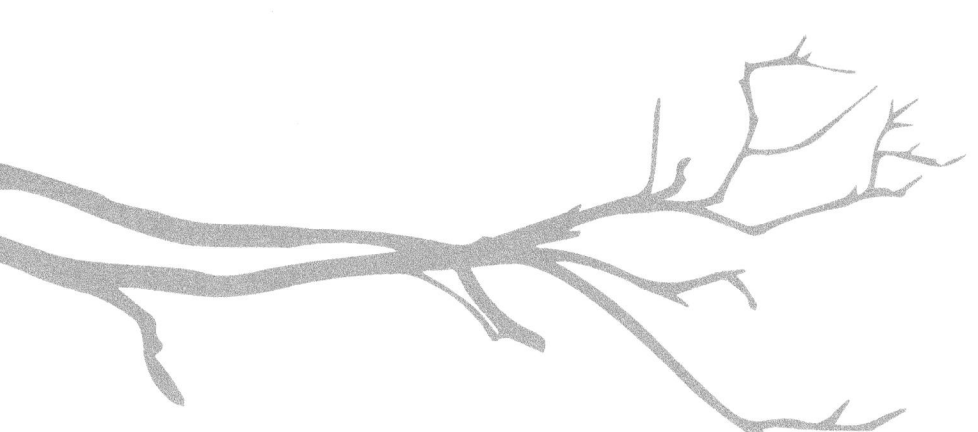

CHAPTER SEVEN

Breaking Family Curses

On December 3, 2008, Cincinnati Judge Robert Ruehlman sentenced an accused gang member to six months in jail for cussing. The judge cited him for contempt and said, "You don't say (bleep bleep) in the courtroom." The very next day an attorney made the same mistake in Judge Ruehlman's courtroom, calling the opposing lawyer "a (bleeping) liar," and the judge sentenced him to six months in jail. "I had to give him six months because I gave the other guy six months," the judge said. (Kimball Perry, "Another in jail for cussing," news.Cincinnati.com, 12-5-2008)

Our words can get us in trouble.

The Bible says: *"Death and life are in the power of the tongue."* - **Proverbs 18:21**

What is a curse?

Words, once spoken, cannot be reversed. Such is the power behind a curse. A curse is any expressed wish that some form of adversity or misfortune will befall or attach to one or more persons, a place, or an object.[7] It is a solemn utterance intended to invoke a supernatural power to inflict harm or punishment on someone or something.

Family Curses

It is believed that the sins of an ancestor can be passed down to his future offspring. This is what is referred to as a family or generational curse. According to The Gospel Coalition, a "family or a generational curse describes the cumulative effect on a person of things that their ancestors did, believed, or practiced in the past, and a consequence of an ancestor's actions, beliefs, and sins being passed down." Examples of generational curses are divorce, miscarriages, poverty, mental illness and barrenness.

The primary route through which curses are released is the mouth. The Bible reveals to us the enormous power embedded in the tongue. The Book of James says: *"Even so the tongue is a little member, and boasteth great things. Behold, how great a matter a little fire kindleth! And the tongue is a fire, a world of iniquity: so is the tongue among our members, that it defileth the whole body, and setteth on fire the course of nature; and it is set on fire of hell"* (James 3:5-6). Words said out of annoyance make many people subject to bondage, affliction, and torment by the supernatural powers backing up the evil utterances that were made.

Nowadays, parents heap curses on their children out of annoyance. Most times, this may be triggered by the fact that the children offended the parent, and out of anger, a curse was pronounced. This has been an ages-long practice. In the Bible, Noah cursed his grandson Canaan for the iniquity of his father Ham. Over time, the curses become the initiator of a streak of unpleasant events in descendants' lives and experiences. When a curse is placed on an individual, it may either manifest immediately or, most times, later in the future.

Many people are not successful in life and behave the way they do because of the actions of their parents that have turned to curses over them. There is an account of a family in Switzerland that inherited a

---

[7] Trait: Curse | vndb. https://vndb.org/i819

curse from an atheist grandfather, a man who had written a book expressing contempt for Christianity. All of his children were born with crippled legs or became crippled by way of accidents later in life. Some of his children were mentally disabled, as were some of his grandchildren. There was a general moodiness and depression in all of his descendants, and all of them became professed atheists. Such negative patterns are often seen in the descendants of those who take sides against God. Forces of evil take over their lives. [8]

The pattern sanction is quite common. Some of the evil ancestral strongholds and curses one should pray against include:

- Curses against excelling in life.
- Curses of sickness and infirmities.
- Curses of failure at the breakthrough.
- Curses of near-success syndrome.
- Curses of having to borrow to live.
- Transfer of ancestral difficulties.
- Covenants of dedication to idols.
- Sudden calamity.
- Late marriage.

Family curses are powerful, and sometimes descendants are not aware of the proclamations—the negative words—that their ancestors uttered in annoyance and anger over earlier descendants and by doing so passed down a curse to the whole family line. How much better it would have been for grandparents and great-grandparents to have learned to bless their children instead!

Some curses are placed on some families because of what they did to some people who are not even related to them. As a result, the curse becomes a generational one, and most people who are affected may be unaware of this curse.

Let's look at a brief example from the Bible and see how some of our fathers placed curses and blessings on their children and people related to them:

---

[8] Page 14 of Healing your family tree by Hampsch John

"Reuben, thou art my firstborn, my might, and the beginning of my strength, the excellency of dignity, and the excellency of power: unstable as water, thou shalt not excel; because thou wentest up to thy father's bed; then defiledst thou it: he went up to my couch. Simeon and Levi are brethren; instruments of cruelty are in their habitations. O my soul, come not thou into their secret; unto their assembly, mine honour, be not thou united: for in their anger they slew a man, and in their selfwill they digged down a wall. Cursed be their anger, for it was fierce; and their wrath, for it was cruel: I will divide them in Jacob, and scatter them in Israel."-**Genesis 49:3-7**

This is a good example of what an ancestor did to a child through the power of words (a curse). Reuben was stripped of power, excellence, prominence and eminence by those words. One word spoken by a forefather can have adverse effects on many generations to come in that bloodline. Following the narrative, it took Moses many years after to break this curse on Reuben's lineage. As you pray for deliverance from evil ancestral strongholds and covenants, break and disempower any word, curse or limiting utterance that has been spoken against you and your family in the past.

All the ancestral curses listed above to be prayed against and rebuked may have been passed on from generation to generation from your forefathers' days. Most of these things are obvious to us in our daily lives, but we might never acknowledge that we have had a curse placed on our family due to what our ancestors did in the past.

Being spiritual and born again makes you alert to afflictions and oppressions that have been inflicted on your family from generation to generation. It helps you discern what is not supposed to be in your life and gives you the ability to reject it all.

Sometimes Christians pray to God for blessings and favors, and oftentimes God answers our prayer requests and sends help to us. However, due to some demonic spiritual force entangled in your life without your knowledge, there may be a delay in your reception of God's response to your petition. This may sometimes result in Christians blaming God for not answering their prayers and making their lives miserable. God is not a wicked God. He gave us his Holy Spirit to help us discern when we are inflicted by an evil spirit. But most times we pay no attention because we think the afflictions are too small to be the work of a spirit in action.

Think about this:

The opposite of a curse is a blessing. Several instances in the Bible record parents releasing generational blessings over their children. These blessings continued for generations. Think how glorious your life could be in the absence of family curses.

Let's look at some of God promises to his sons and daughters who obeyed him and were pleasing to him:

"I will make you into a great nation, and I will bless you; I will make your name great, and you will be a blessing. I will bless those who bless you, and whoever curses you I will curse; and all peoples on earth will be blessed through you." -**Genesis 12:2-3 (NIV)**

"When Abram was ninety-nine years old, the Lord appeared to him and said, 'I am God Almighty; walk before me faithfully and be blameless. Then I will make my covenant between me and you and will greatly increase your numbers.'" -**Genesis 17:1-2 (NIV)**

"Abraham will surely become a great and powerful nation, and all nations on earth will be blessed through him." -**Genesis 18:18 (NIV)**

"I will make your descendants as numerous as the stars in the sky and will give them all these lands, and through your offspring all nations on earth will be blessed." -**Genesis 26:4 (NIV)**

"And God said to him, 'I am God Almighty; be fruitful and increase in number. A nation and a community of nations will come from you, and kings will be among your descendants.'" -**Genesis 35:11 (NIV)**

"Now Joseph and all his brothers and all that generation died, but the Israelites were exceedingly fruitful; they multiplied greatly, increased in numbers and became so numerous that the land was filled with them." -**Exodus 1:6-7 (NIV)**

"The Lord your God has increased your numbers so that today you are as numerous as the stars in the sky. May the Lord, the God of your ancestors, increase you a thousand times and bless you as he has promised!" -**Deuteronomy 1:10-11 (NIV)**

"He will love you and bless you and increase your numbers. He will bless the fruit of your womb, the crops of your land—your grain, new wine and olive oil—the calves of your herds and the lambs of your flocks in the land he swore to your ancestors to give you." -**Deuteronomy 7:13 (NIV)**

"Your servant is here among the people you have chosen, a great people, too numerous to count or number." -**1 Kings 3:8 (NIV)**

"You made their children as numerous as the stars in the sky, and you brought them into the land that you told their parents to enter and possess." -**Nehemiah 9:23 (NIV)**

"The promises were spoken to Abraham and to his seed. Scripture does not say 'and to seeds,' meaning many people, but 'and to your seed,' meaning one person, who is Christ." -**Galatians 3:16 (NIV)**

"And you are heirs of the prophets and of the covenant God made with your fathers. He said to Abraham, 'Through your offspring all peoples on earth will be blessed.' When God raised up his servant, he sent him first to you to bless you by turning each of you from your wicked ways." -**Acts 3:25-26 (NIV)**

"If you belong to Christ, then you are Abraham's seed, and heirs according to the promise." -**Galatians 3:29 (NIV)**

Pray Points

1. Every demonic snake planted in my reproductive organs, catch fire!!!
2. Holy Ghost fire, purge out the evil spirit in my foundation, in the name of Jesus.
3. Heavenly Father, arise on my behalf and correct every error done by my forefathers in the past that is affecting my life in the name of Jesus.
4. Blood of Jesus, purify the land of my dominion in the name of Jesus.
5. I nullify all spoken curses against my family, in the name of Jesus.
6. Inherited generational curses in my father's or mother's house causing unprofitable works in my life, break by fire in the name of Jesus.
7. Altars of the wicked surrounding the children of my family, catch fire in the name of Jesus Christ.
8. I declare and say, "My life and my destiny, you are not designed for stagnation and limitation in Jesus's name."
9. I encircle myself and my family in the blood of Jesus. There shall be no in-roads for demons into my family.

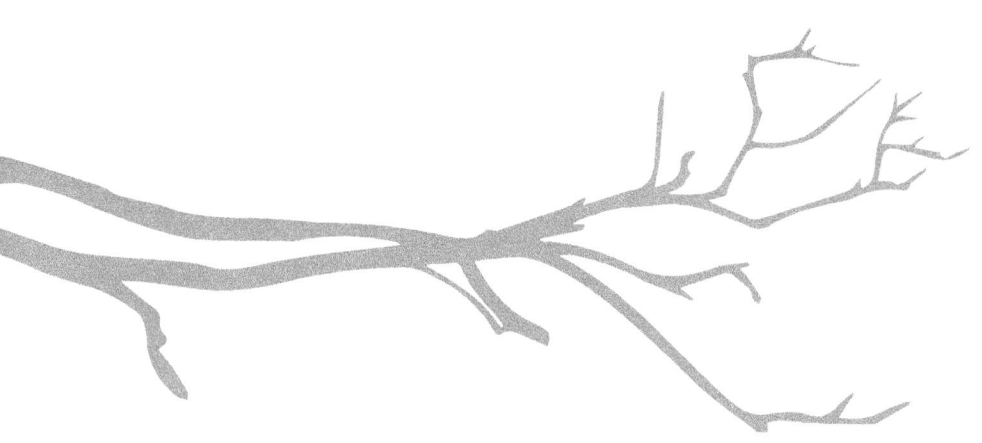

Chapter Eight

Liberation from Evil Garments

> *"No weapon that is formed against thee shall prosper, and every tongue that shall rise against thee in judgement thou shalt condemn. This is the heritage of the servants of the Lord, and their righteousness is of me, saith the Lord."*
> **Isaiah 54:17**

There is no instrument of the enemy, be it witchcraft, disease, sword, persecution, torture, accident or untimely death, that shall have the final say in the life of believers, says the Lord. Every man at creation is clothed in royalty and prestige, but evil ancestral spirits want to exchange this glorious garment with the garments of witchcraft, divorce, setbacks, prostitution, untimely death, disfavor, abandonment, rejection, infirmity (e.g., cancer), shame, disgrace, loneliness, confusion, failure, bad luck, reproach, poverty, and affliction. It takes God's special might to keep our God-given royal covering. It also takes God's might to recover it if evil people have taken it. Whichever state you might be—whether you still have God's glorious covering or whether it's been stolen from you—this chapter is for you. If you still have your royal covering, this chapter will show you the need to continue to ask the Lord to watch over it. If your royal garment has been stolen, this chapter will show you how to trust God for its recovery.

Some time ago there was a man who kept being rejected whenever he tried to secure a big contract. He was a victim of chronic breakthrough-failure, success always seeming to slip through his fingers at the last moment. God led this man to seek deliverance, in the process of which the secret behind his problem was revealed: There was a garment of Hatred/Rejection super-imposed on him in the spirit realm. He prayed and thereafter had a fantastic breakthrough!

Another type of evil garment comes from having somebody who is an evil incarnate in the ancestral line, a custodian of gods or demons who is also a custodian of the family shrine and can fashion a weapon and evil garments of affliction against a family member or a particular family, which is then passed on from generation to generation. One has to sit down and try to discern which garment of affliction has been given to them. Whatever garment has been given to you by your ancestral forefathers, break and dismantle it in the mighty name of Jesus Christ.

Examples of Evil Garments

1. Garment of affliction. This garment introduces suffering, hardship and sorrow into your life. It makes life hard to live and also steals the joy and peace out of living.
2. Garment of disgrace. Nakedness in dreams points to this, either partially or totally. This results in humiliation in life.
3. Garment of poverty and wretchedness. This makes you start borrowing to live, start a business, a project, or even to eat. Proverbs 23:21
4. Garment of ailment. A garment of ailment attracts the diseases of Egypt and manifests as sickness in the physical. Mark 10:50
5. Graveyard clothes. These garments, spiritual and physical, are attached to death. You need to remove these garments just as Lazarus did. John 11:43-44

6. Garment of demotion. Other people less qualified than you catch up with you, pass you, and leave you behind.
7. Garment of slavery. These are garments of profitless hard work with nothing to show for all your efforts.
8. Garment of a vagabond. You will be seeing yourself wandering from one place to the other in your dreams or going to the market and buying nothing. This garment aims at wasting someone's time.
9. Garment of madness. It makes you see mad people in your dreams. It may result in depression and mental illness.
10. Garment of failure. You fail while others succeed. It is the garment of non-achievement.

Deliverance from Evil Ancestral Garments

Joshua he High Priest: Tainted with a Filthy Garment

"And he shewed me Joshua the high priest standing before the angel of the Lord, and Satan standing at his right hand to resist him. And the Lord said unto Satan, The Lord rebuke thee, O Satan; even the Lord that hath chosen Jerusalem rebuke thee: is not this a brand plucked out of the fire? Now Joshua was clothed with filthy garments, and stood before the angel. And he answered and spake unto those that stood before him, saying, Take away the filthy garments from him. And unto him he said, Behold, I have caused thine iniquity to pass from thee, and I will clothe thee with change of raiment. And I said, Let them set a fair mitre upon his head. So they set a fair mitre upon his head, and clothed him with garments. And the angel of the Lord stood by." **-Zechariah 3:1-5**

The dirty and filthy garment is a familiar representation of sin. Joshua the high priest was the leader of the Israelites at the time, and the garment of sin that fell on him subsequently fell on all the people he led too—he stood in their place as their representative. God tells us we should rebuke the devil and all his evil works and garments in our lives.

Notice that this passage shows us that the high priest of God was clothed in a filthy garment. This evil garment is no respecter of title, position, or wealth. In today's churches, pastors and preachers are putting on dirty garments. Some perform godless rituals and use evil powers, while others do vile things such as sleeping with their church members. You cannot live in sin and expect that an evil garment will be taken off you. Be born again and go for deliverance. The Bible says a blind man cannot lead another blind man.

Joseph: Adorned with a Coat Of Many Colors

"Now Israel loved Joseph more than all his children, because he was the son of his old age: and he made him a coat of many colours." **-Genesis 37:3**

The meaning of the coat of many colors is that it foretells a bright future, destiny, and what one will be tomorrow. Like Joseph, we all have a coat of many colors in the eyes of God. This is a sign of the glorious destiny we have. That glorious coat can be robbed, taken away or exchanged by the devil.

"And they took Joseph's coat, and killed a kid of the goats, and dipped the coat in the blood; and they sent the coat of many colors, and they brought it to their father; and said, this have we found: know now whether it be thy son's coat or no. And he knew it, and said, it is my son's coat; an evil beast hath devoured him; Joseph is without doubt rent in pieces." **-Genesis 37:31-33**

Joseph was robbed of his glorious garment, and it was replaced with a prisoner's filthy garment. This is the enemy's plan for your life! He wants to strip you of your God-ordained destiny and replace it with a counterfeit. You must be committed and alert to ward off every one of the enemy's plan to rob you of your garment.

"Then Pharaoh sent and called Joseph, and they brought him hastily out of the dungeon: and he shaved himself, and changed his raiment, and came unto Pharaoh." **-Genesis 41:14**

This verse reveals a divine restoration of Joseph's garment, changed from the garment of pain, suffering and affliction to a glorious garment of promotion and favor. In the mighty name of Jesus Christ, your garment of affliction and suffering will be changed today to a garment of glory and honor.

Blind Bartimaeus: Garment of Sorrow

"And they came to Jericho: and as he went out of Jericho with his disciples and a great number of people, blind Bartimaeus, the son of Timaeus, sat by the highway side begging. And when he heard that it was Jesus of Nazareth, he began to cry out, and say, Jesus, thou son of David, have mercy on me. And many charged him that he should hold his peace: but he cried the more a great deal, Thou son of David, have mercy on me. And Jesus stood still and commanded him to be called. And they call the blind man, saying unto him, be of good comfort, rise; he calleth thee. And he, casting away his garment, rose, and came to Jesus. And Jesus answered and said unto him, what wilt thou that I should do unto thee? The blind man said unto him, Lord, that I might receive my sight. And Jesus said unto him, Go thy way; thy faith hath made thee whole. And immediately he received his sight, and followed Jesus in the way." -**Mark 10:46-52**

As you pray unto God for him to reverse your situation, faith is paramount. Believe and it shall be given unto you. God is all-powerful and he can change every garment of blindness, stagnation, and backwardness in your life and career.

Just like Bartimaeus, who had the garment of sorrow (blindness) but Jesus Christ changed it for him, may it be so in your life in the mighty name of Jesus.

Ruth: A Change of Raiment

"Wash thyself therefore, and anoint thee, and put thy raiment upon thee down to the floor: but make not thyself known unto the man, until he shall have done eating and drinking." -**Ruth 3:3**

As you pray for deliverance, ask God to change your garment that might have been cast upon you or that you might have inherited from your father or mother's side without your knowledge. Rebuke everything that may stain your destiny or your coat of many colors. You should claim a new garment with faith and surely it will be given unto you.

God's Promise of a Garment Exchange

"To appoint unto them that mourn in Zion, to give unto them beauty for ashes, the oil of joy for mourning, the garment of praise for the spirit of heaviness; that they might be called trees of righteousness, the planting of the LORD, that he might be glorified." -**Isaiah 61:3**

In the spiritual realm, there are garments with which God clothes us. These garments are suitable for different kinds of situations. For example, putting on the whole armor of God is suitable for spiritual warfare: *"Put on the whole armor of God that ye may be able to stand against the wiles of the devil"* (Ephesians 6:11). Putting on the armor of Jesus Christ enables us to withstand and resist the devil's agenda. We also need to put on the qualities and virtues of Christ by walking in His ways so that we can showcase Jesus Christ in our lives.

Putting on the garment of praise, gratitude, and joy is the way to counter the spirit of anger, resentment, and heaviness. Harboring resentment in our hearts inhibits our fellowship with God and it blocks our blessings. This resentment can come as a result of putting on the garment of heaviness. In Isaiah 63:1 above, God promises to clothe his people with a garment of praise and take away from them the spirit of heaviness.

Think about this:

A natural garment somewhat determines the prestige a person receives physically. The spiritual garment is what defines the character or success of a person in life. An evil ancestral garment can be fashioned against someone or can be inherited. For example, if a mother was a prostitute, that evil garment can be passed down to her daughter.

Action point:

Man cannot remain naked and unclothed. If through sin one removes the armor of Christ, the devil will immediately fashion an evil garment and clothe him with it. We must avoid sin and its enticement. We must protect our God-given royal garment.

Prayer Points for Removing and Destroying Evil Garments

1. Any beings set to clothe me with an evil garment, may they all be destroyed.
2. Every hand that has taken the assignment of making an evil garment for me, may such hand wither and burn off.
3. Even if they've succeeded in making an evil garment for me, may the Lord set it on fire; it is burnt into ashes and never to be recovered.
4. Every evil garment the enemies have sewn, none of them shall fit me. They are not for me, not for my body.
5. Every load and responsibility that is evil and not from the Lord, I send it back to the sender, I reject it all, and it becomes your portion and not mine in the name of Jesus.
6. Every power that strives with me, to take off my garment of honor, I say no to you. May the Lord raise a standard against you, may the Lord contend with you. You will not have my God-given garment, in the name of Jesus.
7. Anyone that has prepared evil garments for me, in all their forms (beggar garment, or the garments of blindness, infirmity, poverty, disease, untimely death, etc.), may the Lord return them to you; wear them and die with them.
8. Evil garments that I have worn unconsciously, O God, give your angels charge to take them off me, let them be replaced with the best of your garments.
9. Every garment responsible for bringing evil to my life, Lord, set it on fire, let it burn into ashes.
10. Every evil dropped into my life, destiny, and career, Lord, let your blood wash it out of my system.
11. Every strange thing in my body, Lord, search my life, bring all the strange things out, and destroy them all.
12. Every relationship or soul tie with evil kingdoms, the Lord separate me from them all, in the name of Jesus.

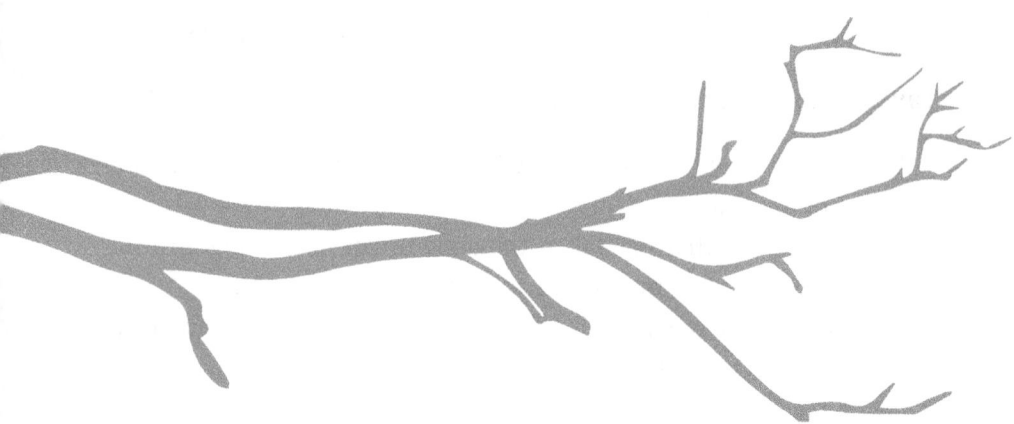

CHAPTER NINE

The Power and Place of Thanksgiving in Deliverance

Matthew Henry, the great Bible commentator, was robbed one day. He wrote in his diary: "Let me be thankful, first, because I was never robbed before. Second, because although they took my wallet, they did not take my life. Third, because although they took my all, it was not much. Fourth, because it was I who was robbed, not I who robbed."

There's always something to be thankful for.

And the act of thanksgiving is a powerful weapon in our deliverance.

Thanksgiving to the Lord

It is Right

Many times we are quick to pray and express our needs, but slow to give thanks to the Lord. But Bible says in Psalm 136:1, *"O give thanks unto the Lord; for he is good: for his mercy endureth for ever."* You see, beloved, thanksgiving acknowledges that God is *"good"* and that he shows his *"mercy"* to us. It acknowledges the unending benefits, favors, and abundant blessings that we receive from God daily. It confesses our dependence on him. In other words, thanksgiving is the right thing to do.

It is Powerful

The Bible says in Psalm 100:4, *"Enter into his gates with thanksgiving, and into his courts with praise: be thankful unto him, and bless his name."* Beloved, we see from this verse that thanksgiving ushers us into the presence of God: We *"Enter into his gates"* and *"courts"* with it, that is, we enter into his presence with it.

And when God's presence comes on the scene, miraculous things happen! You remember the story of Paul and Silas in the Philippian jail in Acts 16. They were thrown into the *"inner prison"* and their feet put in stocks (24), but about midnight they decided to count their blessings and give praise to God instead of complaining. Do you remember what happened when they sang hymns to God? God showed up! Their chains fell off, the jail doors flew open, and the jailer rushed in and brought them out and asked, "What must I do to be saved?" (Acts 16:22-34) Wow! The miraculous took place when Paul and Silas praised because God showed up. The same will happen when you give praise and thanks to God. He will show up on the scene and help you.

Thanksgiving is powerful, especially in times of spiritual warfare. It confuses the enemy, who fully expected to hear us moaning and complaining instead. Thanksgiving in warfare is not telling God what to do, but rather expressing that we believe God knows the best way to win the battle. It lifts our eyes off our circumstances to our God, who is ruler over all. When we praise God, he gives commands to his angels on our behalf. Indeed, thanksgiving is powerful!

It Changes Our Heart

Not only is thanksgiving right and powerful, it also changes and lifts our heart. Thanksgiving erases doubts, builds our trust, and reminds us of God's past victories in history and in our lives.

> *"Be careful for nothing; but in everything by prayer and supplication with thanksgiving let your requests be made known unto God. And the peace of God, which passeth all understanding, shall keep your hearts and minds through Christ Jesus."* - **Philippians 4:6-7**

Beloved, note from these verses that we are invited to pray about *"everything"* that we need, but that *"thanksgiving"* is to accompany our prayers. Thanksgiving should accompany our prayers because it is an expression of faith that God has heard us, cares about us, and will answer us. At the same time, it humbly expresses our complete dependence on him.

Note also that *"peace"* of *"hearts and minds"* is the result of thanksgiving. You see, thanksgiving does an inner work in us, soothing, resting, and strengthening our heart.

Choose Thanksgiving!

When you're fainting and down, about to give up, instead switch to thanksgiving! When it seems like prayer isn't working, switch to thanksgiving! When confused and helpless, switch to thanksgiving! When heaven seems closed, switch to thanksgiving!

Beloved, nobody can stop you from giving thanks—that is, nobody but you. You can always choose to give thanks. And you'll be glad you did. It is right, it is powerful, and it changes the heart.

Think about this:

Thanksgiving is an important part of prayers to God. With a humbled heart, bowed head, lifted heads, opened mouth, we can lift God to act in our favor as we sing his praise.

Actionable points

Thanksgiving in warfare shows how much faith we have in God. In the heat of battle and in the midst of pain, when doubt wants to set in, you should switch to praise. It rekindles hope and moves God's hand for our help.

Prayer Points for Thanksgiving to the Lord

1. Thank you, Lord, for the grace and enablement to be at your service and to still be able to call you Father, in Jesus's name.
2. Thank you, Lord, for protecting me from the snares of the fowler and the noisome pestilence, in Jesus's name.
3. Thank you, Jesus, for your peace that's with me and the good health you have blessed me with, in Jesus's name.
4. Thank you, Lord, for your promises have produced awesome results in my life, in Jesus's name.
5. Thank you for being a shield around me.
6. I thank you, O Lord, because your Word says, *"But my God shall supply all your need according to his riches in glory by Christ Jesus"* (Philippians 4:19).
7. I thank you for giving me glory in the place of reproach and prestige in place of shame, in the name of Jesus.
8. I thank you, O Lord, for the gift of life and your presence in my life, in Jesus's name.
9. Faithful Father, thank you for giving ear to my cries when I'm troubled and for coming to my rescue and help from your holy sanctuary, in the name of Jesus.
10. Thank you, Lord, for revealing deep and secret things to me, in the name of Jesus.
11. Thank you for turning my mourning into joy, giving me beauty for ashes, glory for reproach, and changing my disappointments into appointments.
12. I appreciate you, dear Lord, for saving my soul from the grip of hell and sin, for giving me the opportunity to be called your child. Thank you, dear Jesus.
13. We thank you for you will help us. Strengthen and teach us to wait and trust in you, and not in man or our might, in the name of Jesus.
14. Thank you, for, according to your Word, you will visit my life and uproot everything that is not planted by you, in Jesus's name.

15. Thank you, because you will rule in my marriage, and I will have peace like no other. Thank you for providing the best and right person for me.
16. Thank you, Lord, for shedding your light upon my life and my career.
17. Lastly, thank you, Lord, for your right hand of righteousness will rest on me, it upholds me, it brings me peace and favor, it brings me comfort. I rest in the solace of your hands. Thank you for you will give answers to all that I have prayed about, in Jesus name.

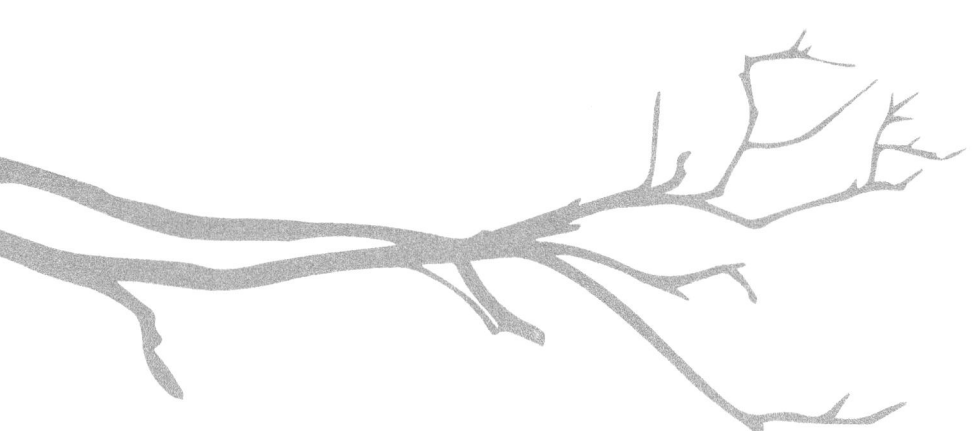

CHAPTER TEN

Engaging the Scriptures for Victory

A woman named Mavis Gustafson Pigford was given a Bible at the Iowa State Fair. A member of the Gideons Bible ministry gave it to her. She put it in her purse. A few days later she was robbed at gunpoint. The assailant shot her in her in the side and she fell to the ground. He then took the wallet from her purse, threw the purse on her head, and shot it! "I felt a dreadful impact," Mavis said. At the hospital, her sister said, "Do you know what saved you, Mavis?" and she handed Mavis the Bible she had put in her purse—and there Mavis saw a bullet lodged in the pages! God's Word had literally saved Mavis' life. (*The Best of Guideposts,* Ideals Publications, 2005, pp. 256-257)

Just as a physical copy of the Bible rescued Mavis from a criminal's attack, so the spiritual presence of God's Word—in our spirit, words, and actions—will rescue us from our spiritual enemy's assaults.

The Power of the Word

When it comes to healing your poisoned family tree, and overcoming the power of witchcraft and every evil force rising against you, the power that resides in the Word of God must be put into operation. And the only one who can do that for you is you! You must be the one to fill your spirit, thoughts, words, and actions with the Word of God.

An Unfailing Weapon

The Word of God is our unfailing weapon when it comes to spiritual warfare. The Bible refers to it as a sharp, double-edged sword:

"For the word of God is alive and active. Sharper than any double-edged sword, it penetrates even to dividing soul and spirit, joints and marrow; it judges the thoughts and attitudes of the heart." **-Hebrews 4:12 (NIV)**

In ancient times, the sword was the main weapon of warfare; it was the soldier's indispensable tool, similar to today's rifle. By giving us his Word to use in our spiritual battles, God is sending us against the enemy fully equipped for victory. Ephesians 6:17 calls the Word of God *"the sword of the Spirit,"* which means it is backed by God himself. The Word is the same Voice that commanded the mountains and seas into existence (Genesis 1). It has the power to break chains and release people from their captives' hands. There is no battle we cannot win with such a weapon on our side.

When we take the truth of God's Word and pray it back to him, we are striking the enemy with that invincible double-edged sword. And the Bible says that God's eternal Word will never return to him empty; it will always accomplish its purpose, always succeed:

"So shall my word be that goeth forth out of my mouth: it shall not return unto me void, but it shall accomplish that which I please, and it shall prosper in the thing whereto I sent it." **-Isaiah 55:11**

It is our unfailing weapon.

A Weapon that Requires Training

No soldier is sent into battle without training to use his weapons effectively. A soldier would spend years learning to wield his sword. Likewise, we need training in the Word to wield *"the sword of the Spirit"* effectively, as Paul wrote to Timothy:

"Study to shew thyself approved unto God, a workman that needeth not to be ashamed, rightly dividing the word of truth." **-2 Timothy 2:15**

For us to defeat the enemy, we must study the Bible diligently. Beloved, for every bondage, challenge, and temptation you may face, there is a specific promise or instruction or insight or command inside the pages of the Book that addresses it. You might say, "But I don't know where to find it." The Book would say to you, *"It is the glory of God to conceal a thing: but the honour of kings is to search out a matter"* (Proverbs 25:2). We are the *"kings"* called to search those matters out. A diligent study of God's Word will open our minds and spirits to receive the necessary truths and wield them against the evil works of the devil.

A Weapon Carried with Honor

As important as it is to understand the Word and its power, it is even more important to walk in obedience to its commands. The Word is the *Spirit's* sword—that is, it belongs to him—and only he can give you the privilege to use it. The privilege is given to those who obey him, to those who carry the sword with honor.

Obedience to God's commands is paramount. When we act contrary to God's mind and instructions, it does not matter how much of God's Word we know and use against the devil; it will not work. If we have used God's Word without success, we should do a heart-check: Are we living in some kind of disobedience? God is not weak, and his Word is not without power. The fault must lie with the one who handled the weapon. A sharp sword handled by an amateur or by an undisciplined person may do more damage to them than to their enemy. Be sure to carry your "sword" with honor.

The Power is Available to You

But when our lives are free from sin, we are free to boldly use the authority in the Word of God to pull down the strongholds of witchcraft and sorcery. That is why I have placed prayers and faith declarations at the end of the chapters, to lead you in releasing the power of God in your behalf. God wants you to gain deliverance and secure victory.

Think about this:

To win and conquer in life, power is needed—extraordinary power at that. It is important to understand that supernatural power comes from only two sources, God or the devil. But God's supernatural power is far above the enemy's—matchless and unconquerable. When we pray God's Word, we pray God's will, and his power is released on our behalf.

Action point

To understand, to know, and to experience the power in the written Word of God, give yourself to studying the Bible daily; meditate over it; and pray with it.

Pray Points

1. Let the thunder, fire and lightning of the Lord scatter all the forces of the enemy in the name of Jesus.
2. Any ritual or sacrifice made for my sake to explore and rid me of my virtues, the sacrifice of Christ and the covenant of his blood destroys it all, in Jesus's name.
3. Lord, let your fire destroy every wicked power using astral travel to get at me.
4. Every mark made upon me to identify me for evil, the blood of Christ washes it off my life and destiny. God's Word says that anyone who has been marked for death shall be set free, and the blood of the lamb sets me free from all evil marks.
5. Every unseen enemy that works at night to carry out evil plans, in my home, my office, and all that surrounds me, planning to subdue and rule over me, the Lord expose you, the fire of the Lord consume you, in Jesus's name.

6. I disconnect and disengage myself completely from every network of evil against my life. Marine, witchcraft, and evil household networks are all broken in Jesus's name.
7. Every human from the dark world, taking the form of animals to manipulate me, at day or night, the sword of the Lord crush you, you're set on fire, and you will be burnt to ashes in Jesus's name.
8. All marine networks taking my virtues and values, such networks are broken.
9. The network of household witches is destroyed. Whatever binds you together is scattered by the thunder of God. You shall never be joined again, in Jesus's name.
10. Every power that is jealous of me, planning to watch my shame and disgrace, shall be disgraced. They shall be put to shame instead, in Jesus's name.
11. Altars of God, arise and fight against all demonic altars, in Jesus's name.
12. Anyone that wants to use my life in exchange for theirs, aiming to cut my life short for their use, may an end come to them, their plans will not be accomplished. I live in good and sound health with long life, in Jesus' name.

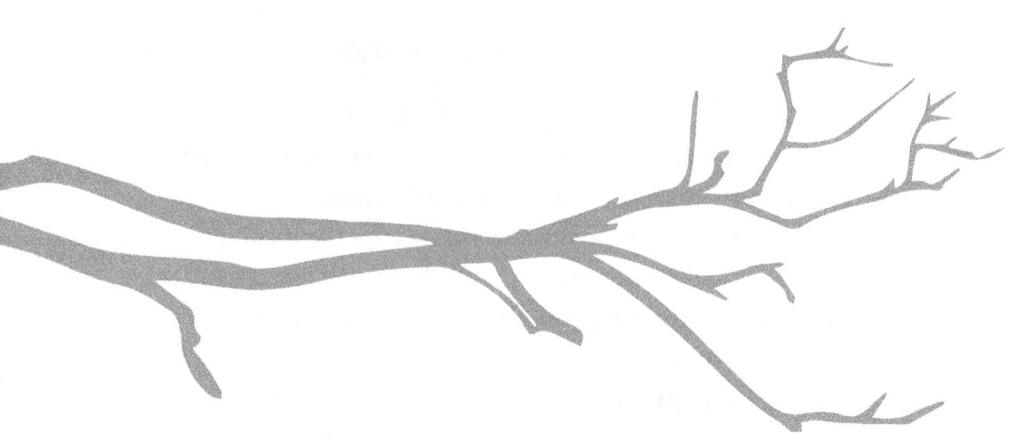

CHAPTER ELEVEN

Scriptural Teachings and Prayers

> "When we depend upon organizations, we get what organizations can do;
> when we depend upon education, we get what education can do;
> when we depend upon man, we get what man can do;
> but when we depend on prayer, we get what God can do."
> Reverend A. C. Dixon

Asking God in Prayer

"*Ask, and it shall be given you; seek, and ye shall find; knock, and it shall be opened unto you*" -**Matthew 7:7**

Everything that we require from God, we should simply ask for through prayer. In difficult situations, prayer is key. When faced with trials and challenges in life, being in despair will not provide a way forward. God listens to your prayers always, and he knows what suits you best. Put your life before God and let him become your defense against your foes.

God has all you can ever request for your safety, good-living, health, prosperity, and so on. With God, you will never lack the good things you need to make headway in life. With prayer, you have an open way of communicating with God whatever is heavy on your chest.

"For I am the Lord, I change not; therefore ye sons of Jacob are not consumed. Even from the days of your fathers ye are gone away from mine ordinances, and have not kept them. Return unto me, and I will return unto you, saith the LORD of hosts. But ye said, wherein shall we return?" **-Malachi 3:6-7**

Our God remains unchangeable. He does not slumber, nor does he backtrack on his Word. You should stand on God's Word and let it guide your day-to-day activities. Pray for God to be your rock, shield, and defense. When this happens, you are on the road to a hitch-free life.

"I shall not die, but live, and declare the works of the LORD." **-Psalm 118:17**

God's blessings to you are innumerable and ever available. Death prevents one from enjoying the countless blessings of God. Therefore, it is important to rebuke the spirit of untimely and sudden death. This provides the avenue to fully live your life to glorify God and share his gospel and goodness with as many souls as possible, and he shall surely reward you.

Through prayers, you develop spiritual resistance to satanic forces around you. Not only that, the plots and schemes of the enemy towards your life are exposed. Therefore, you gain sovereignty over all the devil's work against your life.

God's Promises

Scripture is richly filled with the unwavering and unshaken promises of God to you. Though they may tarry before they are fulfilled, they certainly will manifest at the appointed time.

These promises are meant to keep you forging ahead during your dark days and low moments. Not a portion of the Scriptures will you turn to and not find God's promise to you.

Remember, the Scripture says in Psalm 91:3-4 that *"surely he shall deliver thee from the snare of the fowler, and from the noisome pestilence.*

He shall cover thee with his feathers, and under his wings shalt thou trust: his truth shall be thy shield and buckler."

Similarly, in Isaiah 43:2, God says, *"when thou passest through waters, I will be with thee; and through the rivers, they shall not overflow thee: when thou walkest through the fire, thou shalt not be burned; neither shall the flame kindle upon thee."*

The Book of Job elaborates in chapter 5 and verse 12: *"He disappointeth the devices of the crafty, so that their hands cannot perform their enterprise."* That is God saving you from the crafty—those who pretend to be close to you but instead have evil plans for you.

Likewise, Deuteronomy 31:8 says that *"the LORD himself goes before you and will be with you; he will never leave you nor forsake you. Do not be afraid; do not be discouraged."* This promise assures you that the Lord himself is involved in your business. He is the leading soldier in your battle; therefore, fear is unnecessary. God's got you!

God's favor, protection and goodwill for his people, including you, gives abundant comfort. The Bible says those with God on their side need not worry or fear no matter who is against them. God promises to keep you under his wings for protection from the enemy at all times.

Think about this:

The power, wisdom, and strength of man can do nothing; man's resources lack the potency to loosen the grip of darkness upon your life. So, what do you do? You pray that the eyes of your spiritual understanding be enlightened so that you may understand the hope to which God has called you. The Word of God never fails. His promises stand sure, and God answers prayers. Remember this always, and you will have the upper hand on your adversaries.

Declarations

- Lord, I break all curses directed to me and my family by naysayers. Let your blessings run through all my generations to come.

Shame all my enemies and may they be alive to see as you bless me abundantly, amen.
- God, I take authority by your Word today. I will not fall into the trap of the evil ones. I am seated with Christ in heavenly places far above all principalities and power.
- I shall not die but live to declare the works and salvation of the Lord. I shall live as a witness to God's death and resurrection.
- I am eternally delivered from the snares of fowlers in my family. I shall prosper and be in health.
- My life is committed into God's hands. I submit my life to him and enjoy his leadership. No evil shall come near my tent.
- I walk in the light and the salvation of the Lord. The agenda of the devil fails to materialize in my life.
- By the power of the Holy Ghost actively at work in my life, I shall tread on serpents and not be hurt. I receive the Holy Spirit's help to face and overcome every challenge that lies ahead of me. These challenges shall push me to a higher level of faith rather than bring me down.

Prayer Points for Deliverance from Evil Ancestral Spirits

At this point, you would take charge and open your mouth in aggressive prayers. You know what they say, a closed mouth is a closed destiny. Let's pray:

1. I pray in the name of Jesus that the Holy Ghost fire burn around me and protect me from all troubles, evils, and diseases.
2. I quicken my body, soul, and spirit with the fire of the Holy Spirit in the name of Jesus.
3. Every plan of ancestral attack on my life should cease operation in my life in the name of Jesus.
4. I pray with authority in Jesus' name that every demonic serpent troubling me shall lose its life now in Jesus's name.
5. Every demonic snake planted in my reproductive organs shall be destroyed by the consuming fire that goes before the Lord.

6. I proclaim as a child of God that the flaming sword of Elohim arise immediately and crush the head of the demonic serpent in my body.
7. I pull out every serpent located around my spine, neck, head, nose, ears, stomach, armpits—all parts of my body, down to the feet—and I call the fire of God to burn them, in the name of Jesus. You will find your way out now!
8. I declare a permanent exit of this serpent from my body. I command you to get out now. In the name of Jesus, you will leave now!
9. For all power has been given unto me. You will come out of my life right now! LEAVE NOW! In the name of Jesus.
10. My body is the temple of the Lord; therefore, there is no room for you in the mighty name of Jesus.
11. I destroy ALL the serpent's eggs, the nesting, the festering, and the incubating before they hatch, in the name of Jesus.
12. I release the rod of God to swallow up every demonic serpent that would come up against me in the name of Jesus.
13. Let the fire of God drive out every serpent from my life. (Acts26:3)
14. May the Holy Ghost fire purge me of the evil spirit in my foundation, in the name of Jesus.
15. Father, arise and correct the errors and mistakes made by my forefathers in the past that are affecting my life, in Jesus's name.
16. Every ancestral altar labeled against my name and assigned against my body, soul, and spirit is smashed to dust. I then ask for the blood of Christ to remove my name from it in Jesus's name.
17. I decree that the blood of Jesus Christ sanitize my body, soul and spirit. AMEN! PRAISE THE LORD!

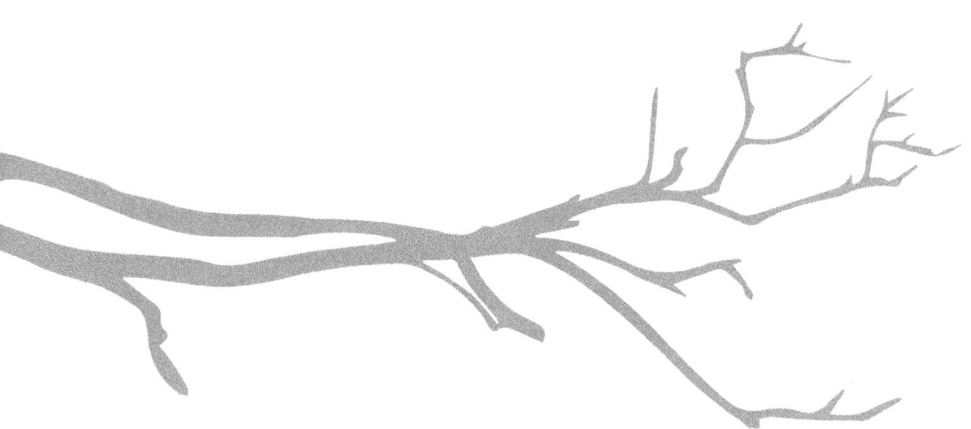

Chapter Twelve

How to Heal Your Poisoned Family Tree

> *"Christ hath redeemed us from the curse of the law, being made a curse for us: for it is written, Cursed is every one that hangeth on a tree."*
> **Galatians 3:13**

Have you ever wondered if you picked up some negative influence from someone in your lineage? Would you like to get the chance to go back and choose the family you belong to? Do you ever get the feeling your family is under a curse? If these questions resonate with you, instead of groping around in darkness or wallowing in self-pity, let me show you the steps to take to heal your poisoned family tree.

This chapter is laden with practical tips that will arrest the influence of a poisoned family tree and have a positive impact on your future.

Examples from History

I began this book (see Introduction) with an account of the great early American preacher Jonathan Edwards' outstanding legacy, how from this one man came some 300 pastors, missionaries, and theological professors; about 120 college professors; 110 attorneys; 60 prominent authors; 30 judges; 14 presidents of universities and colleges; three members of Congress; and one vice-president. *That* is an impressive family tree. There were many factors that went into growing such a lineage, but one I want to be sure to point out is that Edwards was a father who took the time to pray a special blessing on each of his 11 children. The spiritual seeds of faith, hope, and love planted into the hearts of his children blossomed into a glorious family tree producing generations of spiritual fruit.[9]

There are other well-known individuals who were highly successful businessmen who built solid foundations for generations to come, men such as J.D. Rockefeller, F.W. Woolworth, and William Colgate, men who were professing Christians and givers to God's work and charities.

On the flip side, there were other successful men whose lives took a bleak turn at the end. Bob Proctor recounts the story of eight of the world's wealthiest financiers and what became of their lot twenty-five years later. At the end, these men's lives didn't bear any resemblance to the wealth and affluence they once enjoyed. Some died in debt, some committed suicide, some went insane….

What I want you to realize is that it is not only financial crises that can render an individual insolvent. Other issues from your background and ancestral lineage may be the reason for your stagnation and unproductivity. This is what I refer to as a poisoned family tree.

A Poisoned Family Tree

A poisoned family tree is an ancient malady that besieges the descendants of a family from one generation to another. As long as it's in force, members of that family will find things tough. This state of difficulty

---

[9] Perry Stone (2011, pg. 2), *Purging your house, pruning your family tree* (1st ed.) Charisma House

will continue unless they do something about their situation. What does a sick person do? He goes for treatment. Likewise, as one who is besieged with an ancient family tree poisoning, you must set yourself up for healing.

One of the first keys to deliverance is knowledge. You must first know who your adversary is and the schemes through which he has beguiled you. The prophet Isaiah said, *"my people are gone into captivity, because they have no knowledge: and their honourable men are famished, and their multitude dried up with thirst"* (Isaiah 5:13). The prophet Hosea went further to proclaim, *"My people are destroyed for lack of knowledge"* (Hosea 4:6).

This is to show that without accurate knowledge, it might be difficult to get the deliverance and healing we need. Do you realize that everybody has a pattern they follow in their families—from their ancestors—often which they have no clue about?

Normally, every child takes after their parents—physically, spiritually, emotionally, and otherwise. Perhaps someone has told you, "Hey! You talk like your dad." Or, "You resemble your mom." Now, this is God's biological design, that we resemble our ancestors. In like manner, sin is passed down from generation to generation.

What have you come to accept that has become a lens through which you view the world? Perhaps you were born to see your family practicing diabolism. For instance, some tribes believe that when their first daughter wants to marry, sacrifices must be made to the gods for protection and fruitfulness. The misdeeds of ancestors can speak against future generations for years to come if not properly addressed. These and more are some of the poisons in the family tree.

Why do I call these influences poisons? Because they contaminate the original design of God for the family and cause those who practice them to suffer the aftermath of their ignorance.

A story was told by Rebecca Linder Hintze[10] of a young married woman who cut off both ends of a ham as she wanted to prepare it for dinner. As she cut off both ends and put it in a pan, her husband re-

---

[10] *Healing your family history: 5 steps to break free of destructive patterns.* Linder Hintz:

quested to know why she did so. Then she told him, "It makes it taste better."

Subsequently, she gave the process a thought and tried to figure out why she cut off both ends of the ham. So, she reached out to her mother who'd taught her how to cook. Then she asked, "Why did you tell me to cut off the ends of the ham?" Her mother, puzzled, replied, "I'm not sure, but I know it makes it enhance the taste, and my mother used to do the same."

Because she wasn't satisfied with her mother's response, she went on to question her grandmother about it: "Why do we cut off the ends of the ham?" Her nana retorted, "Because it won't fit in my saucepan otherwise."

All along this young woman had believed that pruning the edges of the ham was done to enrich its flavor, when in fact the practice had originated just because her grandmother had a smaller pan! As soon as the young woman learned the truth, she checked the size of her frying pan and realized it could be done differently—a whole piece of meat would fit—and so she changed her actions and the family got more ham to eat.

Just like that young woman, we have inherited traits and dogmas from our forefathers, which we religiously adhere to, often without understanding why.

Although these beliefs may have worked for some people, they don't usually make sense for us. And unlike the humorous ham tradition, some of the practices and patterns we have inherited can have dire consequences in the lives of generations of people. They can poison our family tree.

How to Heal Your Family Tree

So, how do you heal yourself and your tree? Here are the steps:

Understand Your Victory In Christ!

This is the starting point for all healing. The Scripture at the head of this chapter, Galatians 3:13, reveals that Christ has delivered us from the curse. This is a part of the legal benefit of what Christ did for us on the cross—he took our curse upon himself. This does not automatically mean that the poison in your family tree no longer has a hold on you.

What this means is that now you have divinely legal ground on which you can stand and enforce your liberty. Whereas in the past you had nothing with which you could stand against the hold of evil in your ancestry, now you have the confidence and assurance that comes from standing in the finished work of Christ. God's word declares that you have been freed from the curse! That is the solid ground on which you stand.

As you come to the understanding of this truth, you'll be enabled to wage a good warfare. Not out of fear and ignorance but from a heart of understanding! When you've come to know your kingdom rights made available in Christ, you'll be able to face the adversary, and by the application of the Word break down every stronghold rising against you, and you'll be able to obtain your healing.

Pray!

"For we wrestle not against flesh and blood, but against principalities, against powers, against the rulers of the darkness of this world, against spiritual wickedness in high places." **-Ephesians 6:12**

One of the greatest weapons for our warfare is prayer. Prayer is to the believer what a drug is to the sick. This means that it's one of the cures for life's problems—including ancestral poison in the family.

Once you've identified the venom in the family tree, rise against it on your knees! The Bible clearly states that the prayer of the righteous availeth much (James 5:16). And God doesn't lie! He has promised to deliver you from the devil's cage of darkness if you're willing to separate from the wrongdoings of your family.

"Wherefore come out from among them, and be ye separate, saith the Lord, and touch not the unclean thing; and I will receive you." **-1 Corinthians 6:17**

In truth, God will not force you out of your relationship with the devil. However, he'll present you with choices and allow you to decide. Now, the ball in your court! Choose!

Renounce And Be Refined

"If we confess our sins, he is faithful and just to forgive us our sins, and to cleanse us from all unrighteousness." **-1 John 1:9**

To confess means to take a deliberate action of openly conceding wrongdoing. You must, first of all, admit that everything's not okay, and you'd like it otherwise. Understand that confession will expose the poison in your family tree.

It will bring it to light, and prove that you're ready to renounce it. Evil is stronger in the dark, in secret. And the truth is, usually we don't realize that we're gradually dying in our father's mistakes until they're brought to light—from our mouths.

Scripture reveals that the Word of God is light. It says, *"Then spake Jesus again unto them, saying, I am the light of the world: he that followeth me shall not walk in darkness, but shall have the light of life"* (John 8:12), You can only renounce the evil you were born into by dealing with it through the Word of God.

When you use the Word to counter what your ancestors designed, you allow the Word to flow through you and refine you into a New Man. The assurance is, *"Therefore if any man be in Christ, he is a new creature: old things are passed away; behold, all things are become new."* **-2 Corinthians 5:17**

Jesus is the Word of God. So, if you allow him in your heart, you have all it takes to fight against the poison in your bloodline because his blood will purify and heal you of every ancestral venom.

National and ancestral repentance was practiced by many of the Old Testament saints. Examples are Daniel and Nehemiah. When Nehemiah heard of the calamity that befell Jerusalem, he went into fasting, prayer, mourning, and repentance.

In Nehemiah's words, *"And it came to pass, when I heard these words, that I sat down and wept, and mourned certain days, and fasted, and prayed before the God of heaven."* **-Nehemiah 1:4**

Nehemiah's personal act of prayer and repentance triggered the deliverance that subsequently came to Jerusalem through him. Likewise, Daniel, when he *"understood by books"* the number of years the children of Israel were to spend in captivity, went to God in prayers and supplications, with fasting, sackcloth, and ashes (Daniel 9:2-3).

In Daniel's words, *"I prayed unto the LORD my God, and made my confession, and said, O Lord, the great and dreadful God, keeping the covenant and mercy to them that love him, and to them that keep his commandments; We have sinned, and have committed iniquity, and have done wickedly, and have rebelled, even by departing from thy precepts and from thy judgments."* **-Daniel 9:4-5**

Like Nehemiah, Daniel also sought the face of God not just for himself but for the entire nation of Israel. He beseeched the Lord to deliver them from the sins of their ancestors. He confessed and renounced the wicked acts and legacy left in their family tree. As a result of this, God hearkened to his prayer and responded with grace. There was healing and restoration.

Seek The Prophet's Intervention

"And the men of the city said unto Elisha, Behold, I pray thee, the situation of this city is pleasant, as my lord seeth: but the water is naught, and the ground barren. And he said, Bring me a new cruse, and put salt therein. And they brought it to him. And he went forth unto the spring of the waters, and cast the salt in there, and said, Thus saith the LORD, I have healed these waters; there shall not be from thence any more death or barren land. So the waters were healed unto this day, according to the saying of Elisha which he spake." **-2 Kings 2:19-22**

The prophet is God's mouthpiece on the earth. In the story above, the people lived in a good location but had bad water and therefore the land was unfruitful. These blights were outward symptoms of an ancient proclamation upon that land. The land was suffering from a poisoned genealogy. Thankfully, the men of that land understood that its problem went beyond the natural and so sought help from Elisha—God's prophet. As a man of God, Elisha was able to bring a permanent solution to the ill of the land.

Seeking out a prophet to administer God's counsel and deliverance from your ills and hurts is a wise step to take. Many times, the prophets are privy to information you may not have and so can be of great help, just like Elisha was to the people of Jericho.

Prayer

1. Dear father, I thank you for exposing the devil and his works in my family. The Bible says that I'm free from the curse of the law. Therefore, I decree and declare that I don't belong to any evil ancestry.
2. I ask that the blood of Jesus purify me from every sin that I've committed against you.
3. Take over my life, my family, and my all.
4. I renounce every evil covenant that my family may have entered into, in Jesus' name.
5. I break the power of darkness over my life.
6. I come against every poison in my bloodline; rather, I walk in the blessings of Abraham.
7. My family is free and free indeed, in Jesus' name.
8. I stand on the finished works of Christ for me! Christ has made me free!
9. Every spiritual intelligence holding me down through ignorance, I disarm you today in the name of Jesus.
10. I confess and renounce every evil act in my family tree that is responsible for the poisoning in my family tree. Amen.

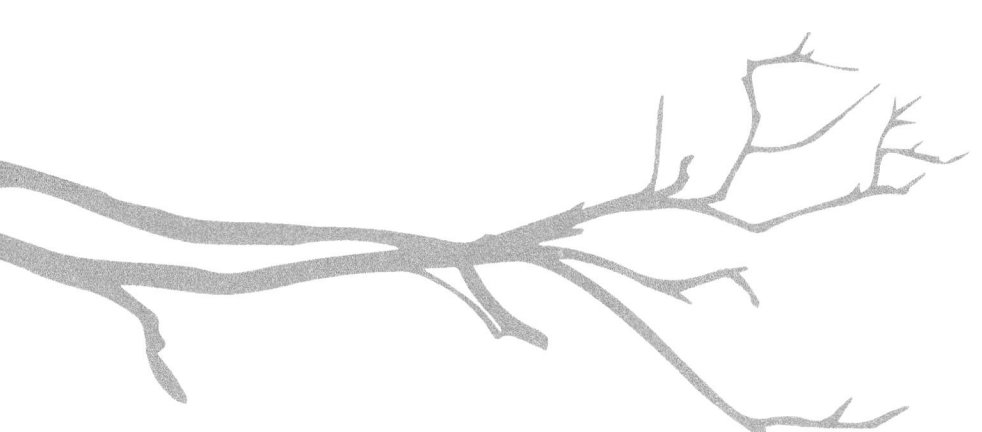

CHAPTER THIRTEEN

Aggressive Prayer Based on the Scriptures

In the midst of a California wildfire crisis several years ago, Christian recording artist Rebecca St. James had to flee her home as the blazes closed in. Urgent prayers were asked for her on Facebook: "Prayers needed! Rebecca was just evacuated from her home in CA due to a wildfire." Later came the report that her home had been spared: "A tree in our front yard was burnt and a water pipe burst, but our house is ok! Sounds like the fire came right to our back fence. It's a total miracle cause the wind changed right when the fires were about to take over our house. You can see the proof when you look at where the fire stopped, three feet from our back fence. The fire was a two-three story wall of flame, only meters away from our home!" Those urgent Facebook prayers had been prayed just in time! (Jeannie Law, "Rebecca St James' Home Spared as California Wildfires Stop Just Feet From House; Singer Asks Fans to 'Please Pray For Us'," breathecast.com (5/15/14)

There's a time for urgent, aggressive prayers!

Aggressive Prayer

Hannah

The Apostle Paul instructed the Ephesian church to *"pray in the Spirit on all occasions **with all kinds of prayers** and requests"* (Ephesians 6:18, NIV, emphasis added). In other words, there is more than one kind of prayer. There are prayers of praise, prayers of confession of sin, prayers of meditation and listening to the Spirit, prayers of fellowship, and so forth. And there comes a time for *aggressive prayer!*

Difficult circumstances often bring about the need for aggressive prayer, those times when you offer up requests and intercessions to God fiercely, combatively, urgently. Those moments when your hope seems bleak and your enemy victorious, the only remedy is to turn to God in aggressive prayer.

Aggressive prayer does not necessarily mean loud, raw-throated prayer. An aggressive prayer can be a quiet, even silent prayer. An aggressive prayer is not about the amount of noise you make, but about being stirred up in your inner man. Hannah's aggressive prayer to have a son and lose her disgrace was a silent prayer:

[10] *"**In her deep anguish Hannah prayed to the Lord**, weeping bitterly.* [11] *And she made a vow, saying, 1Lord Almighty, if you will only look on your servant's misery and remember me, and not forget your servant but give her a son, then I will give him to the Lord for all the days of his life, and no razor will ever be used on his head.'*

[12] *As she kept on praying to the Lord, Eli observed her mouth.* [13] ***Hannah was praying in her heart, and her lips were moving but her voice was not heard.***" -1 Samuel 1:10-13 **(NIV, emphasis added)**

Hannah made her request known to God the provider in an intense spiritual communication that was silent, and her prayer was answered: her son Samuel, who would become one of Israel's most important prophets, was born.

The Widow

In Luke 18:1-8, Jesus told the parable of a judge and a widow. She prayed the judge to defend and grant her justice from her adversary, but the judge declined. The widow never stopped until her wish was granted. The widow's aggressive prayer was demonstrated by her *persistence*. Jesus told this parable to teach us to pray without ceasing and not lose hope when our prayers have not been answered yet.

Jesus

Jesus prayed aggressively in the Garden of Gethsemane.

"And being in an agony he prayed more earnestly: and his sweat was as it were great drops of blood falling down to the ground." **-Luke 22:44**

He was in agony, so he prayed fervently to his Father. He needed to help concerning his imminent death. His prayer was so aggressive that it yield drops of blood from his body!

The Church and Peter

"So Peter was kept in prison, but the church was earnestly praying to God for him." **-Acts 12:5 (NIV)**

When Peter was arrested for the sake of the gospel, the church prayed for him *"earnestly,"* that is, with aggressive passion. And what happened? He was released—a great miracle that surprised even those praying for him.

Aggressive Prayer Based on Scripture

What makes prayer rich and effective—that is, bringing answers—is when it is founded on Scripture, when it is developed straight from God's words found in the Bible. Nothing has more spiritual power than God's Word being prayed out loud by a believer. Following are two wonderful psalms to base your prayers to your Father on today. Individualize these prayers by inserting your own name in the applicable places.

Psalm 140:1-13

¹ *Deliver me, O Lord, from the evil man: preserve me from the violent man;*
    ² *Which imagine mischiefs in their heart; continually are they gathered together for war.*

³ They have sharpened their tongues like a serpent; adders' poison is under their lips. Selah.

⁴ Keep me, O Lord, from the hands of the wicked; preserve me from the violent man; who have purposed to overthrow my goings.

⁵ The proud have hidden a snare for me, and cords; they have spread a net by the wayside; they have set gins for me. Selah.

⁶ I said unto the Lord, Thou art my God: hear the voice of my supplications, O Lord.

⁷ O God the Lord, the strength of my salvation, thou hast covered my head in the day of battle.

⁸ Grant not, O Lord, the desires of the wicked: further not his wicked device; lest they exalt themselves. Selah.

⁹ As for the head of those that compass me about, let the mischief of their own lips cover them.

¹⁰ Let burning coals fall upon them: let them be cast into the fire; into deep pits that they rise not up again.

¹¹ Let not an evil speaker be established in the earth: evil shall hunt the violent man to overthrow him.

¹² I know that the Lord will maintain the cause of the afflicted and the right of the poor.

¹³ Surely the righteous shall give thanks unto thy name: the upright shall dwell in thy presence.

Psalm 91:1-12
¹ He that dwelleth in the secret place of the Most High shall abide under the shadow of the Almighty.

² I will say of the Lord, He is my refuge and my fortress: my God; in him will I trust.

³ Surely he shall deliver thee from the snare of the fowler, and from the noisome pestilence.

⁴ He shall cover thee with his feathers, and under his wings shalt thou trust: his truth shall be thy shield and buckler.

⁵ Thou shalt not be afraid for the terror by night; nor for the arrow that flieth by day;

⁶ Nor for the pestilence that walketh in darkness; nor for the destruction that wasteth at noonday.

⁷ A thousand shall fall at thy side, and ten thousand at thy right hand; but it shall not come nigh thee.

⁸ Only with thine eyes shalt thou behold and see the reward of the wicked.

⁹ Because thou hast made the Lord, which is my refuge, even the most High, thy habitation;

¹⁰ There shall no evil befall thee, neither shall any plague come nigh thy dwelling.

¹¹ For he shall give his angels charge over thee, to keep thee in all thy ways.

¹² They shall bear thee up in their hands, lest thou dash thy foot against a stone.

Instances When You Need Deliverance

Deliverance breaks evil yokes, damages the works of Satan in your life, opens up your locked doors and destiny, and reinstates everything that the devil has stolen from you. In summary, to be delivered means to have your lost fortunes and glory restored.

You need deliverance:

- If you are having constant scary dreams and nightmares.
- If you have ever participated in an ungodly relationship.
- If you have regular or irregular involuntary movement of body parts such as legs, hands, eyes, or if you feel unknown things walking or moving inside you.
- If you have emotional disturbances.
- If you hear voices from unseen beings.
- If you are operating under evil ancestral covenants and curses.
- If you suffer an unexplainable family breakdown.
- If evil spirits constantly attack you.
- If you have visited witches or wizards for spells or enchantments.

Ancestral Witchcraft

Ancestral witchcraft is a witchcraft tradition that focuses heavily on connecting to one's ancestors spiritually or through magic. The consequences of ancestral witchcraft are experienced in all generations in a lineage unless it is broken.

Once you are delivered and born again, do not return to the activities you have forsaken, for that would pave the way for the devil to attack you again and place on you the burden of oppression, bondage, and affliction. When you keep yourself free from those past activities, your life will stay above every affliction or torment.

"Surely there is no enchantment against Jacob, neither is there any divination against Israel: according to this time it shall be said of Jacob and of Israel, what hath God wrought!" -**Numbers 23:23**

Starting today, use Psalm 71:4 to pray against any enchantment of witchcraft done against your life and that of your family and bloodline in the past and in the present:

"Deliver me, O my God, out of the hand of the wicked, out of the hand of the unrighteous and cruel man." -**Psalm 71:4**

Eternal Safety in Christ

"Whoever dwells in the shelter of the Most High will rest in the shadow of the Almighty." -**Psalm 91:1 (NIV)**

As a vessel of the Most High, the kingdom of the evil one cannot stand against you. You are more than a conqueror and kept safe in the cleft of the rock. The enemies will fall into the traps and snares they set for you. They will even turn against one another in a fury. Witches, sorcerers, enchanters, and magicians will lose track of your progress.

Dwelling in the shadow of the almighty God provides you heavenly immunity and security from evil ancestral powers, strongholds, and covenants. Their criticisms and accusations will hold no water because you have Jesus as your advocate, and His blood speaks freedom.

Need you be reminded that through Jesus Christ, you have power over every tongue that rises against you in judgment? This and others privileges are your heritage in Christ. Once more, the pestilence that comes with this age will stay far from you, even the Coronavirus.

"Let them be as chaff before the wind: and let the angel of the LORD chase them. Let their way be dark and slippery: and let the angel of the LORD persecute them." **-Psalm 35:5-6**

Take note of this promise of God. Your life is founded on the eternal rock of ages. Hence, your enemies will blow away like the chaff. Then, you will bask in a long, healthy, stable, and successful life. Now say to yourself God's word in Psalm 118 and verse 17, *"I shall not die, but live, and declare the works of the LORD."* Those who wish you dead will die in your place.

Think about this:

There is nothing under the sun that can come to exist except through God's word declared in prayers. When your prayers seem not to yield results, become aggressive about it. Aggressiveness in prayer accelerates the level at which your request is being processed. It is a mixture of the living Word of God with the stirring of your spirit.

At this stage of your life, leaning totally on God is what is required of you. Remember God's Word in Jeremiah 17:5: *"Cursed is the one who trusts in man, who draws strength from mere flesh and whose heart turns away from the LORD."*

There is safety nowhere else and in no one else. Only Jesus is your eternal stronghold, the rock in which you can hide. By trusting in God and His Word, no trouble can get to you.

Prayer Points for Deliverance from Ancestral Witchcraft Powers

1. Lord, thank you for the gift of life. Let me experience and enjoy the beauty of life in Jesus's name.
2. Father, I ask that you empower my spirit to fight back against my enemies in aggressive prayers in the name of Jesus.
3. All tools used by the evil ones to place surveillance upon my life are destroyed. They are set on fire right now in Jesus' name.

4. I pray that God rises in his majesty and scatters my enemies and burns them with his fire roundabout. It is high time they stopped assaulting my destiny.
5. I am covered with the precious blood of Jesus. I erect a fence of safety around me and my household.
6. Any witch, soothsayer, seer, or whosoever that has decided to embark on a journey against my life is pulled down and will not return in the name of Jesus.
7. All programs designed to mess up my life are canceled.
8. Meetings held to drag my destiny in the mud are disrupted.
9. My glory will shine brighter and brighter by God's grace.
10. I receive the spiritual strength to pray. I won't grow weary.
11. My safety is certain in Christ Jesus.
12. I am set free from every spiritual union, alliance, and bond with familiar spirits in the name of Jesus Christ.
13. I am the head and not the tail.
14. My virtues are kept safe in Christ. I shall not lack but enjoy the abundant blessings of my dear God and Father in Jesus' name. Amen!

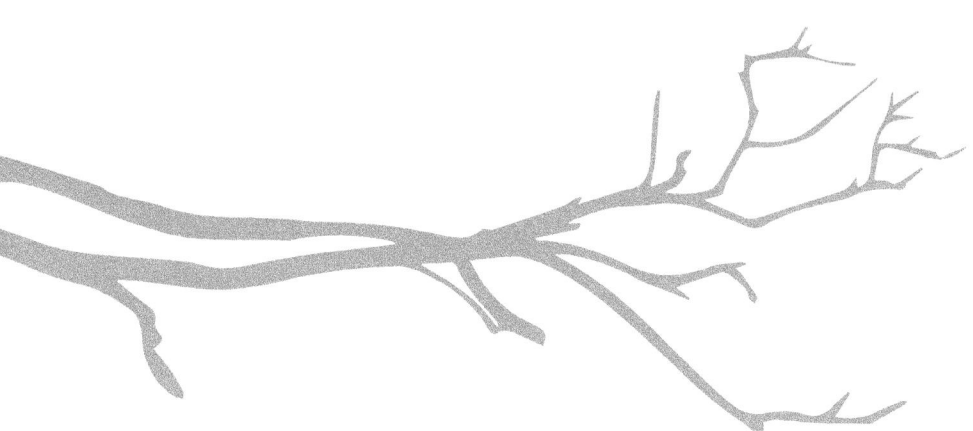

CHAPTER 14

Prayers for Revoking and Severing Soul Ties and Contracts

> *"And don't you realize that if a man joins himself to a prostitute, he becomes one body with her? For the Scriptures say, "The two are united into one."*
> **1 Corinthians 6:16 (NLT)**

Soul Ties

A soul tie refers to a spiritual connection between two people. It occurs when two souls are tied together in the spiritual realm and it can either be a legitimate or an illegitimate connection between them.

Soul bonds can be initiated in diverse ways. However, one striking way to initiate a soul tie is through sexual relations. It is possible to form godly and ungodly connections when a man and woman have sex. Interestingly, if intimacy is a connection between a married couple, such connection leads to a godly tie. But if it occurs between unmarried folks, they are connected in an ungodly tie.

Another possible way of establishing a soul tie is through close relationships. This involves being obsessed with and/or extremely fond of and passionate about a person or a group. An example of this is seen between David and Jonathan.

"As soon as he had finished speaking to Saul, **the soul of Jonathan was knit to the soul of David,** *and Jonathan loved him as his own soul."* -1Samuel 18:1

A soul tie can also be established through agreements, vows and commitments. The Bible declares: *"If a man vows a vow to the LORD, or swears an oath to bind himself by a pledge, he shall not break his word. He shall do according to all that proceeds out of his mouth."* -**Numbers 30:2**

When you make a vow, you are committing yourself to be held accountable for fulfilling the vow. A vow that you make exerts a level of influence on your soul till you fulfill it. This was why King Solomon exhorted in the Book of Ecclesiastes: *"When you vow a vow to God, do not delay paying it, for he has no pleasure in fools. Pay what you vow. It is better that you should not vow than that you should vow and not pay."* -**Ecclesiastes 5:4-5**

We initiate soul ties when we partake of any of these mentioned above. And having your soul tied with another may later come to haunt you if not properly addressed. You must learn to consciously revoke and sever every soul tie and contract that surrounds your life.

As you begin to speak the words of the prayers provided below to revoke and sever every soul tie, God will proceed to work out your freedom, in Jesus' name!

Revoking Ancestral Vows, Pledges, Oaths, and Promises

Pray the following prayers to sever all evil soul ties in your life. Pray them all "in Jesus' name."

In Jesus' name,

- I come into the court of the Most High with my worship and praise!

- I come into God's court to renounce useless evil vows, oaths, pledges, and promises that I made and are binding, limiting, and opposing God's will and purpose in my life.
- Yahweh Elohim! My sole purpose is to serve and honor you. So, I begin to align myself to your divine mandate, purpose, and plan.
- I stand in the blood of Jesus before the throne of the Most High and let the blood of Jesus speak on my behalf to atone for all my sins.
- I call upon the Holy Spirit to be my witness and Jesus my advocate today as I renounce and revoke all useless vows, pledges, oaths, and promises that have a hold on my life.
- I break all vows, pledges, promises and oaths in my family, lineage, genetics, and bloodline that are directly or indirectly affecting my life.
- Lord, I want to be made whole! Jesus Christ, rescue and deliver me today so that I can marvelously fulfill my destiny.
- I am free from all evil soul ties and contracts now! AMEN!

Affirmations of Freedom in Christ

Declare the following affirmations as you NOW walk in limitless liberty!

- I AM a child of God!
- I AM chosen!
- I AM adopted!
- I AM forgiven!
- I AM a royal priest!
- I AM co-heir with Christ!
- I AM God's masterpiece!
- I AM courageous!
- I AM God's friend!
- I AM accepted by God!
- I AM capable!
- I AM blessed!

- I AM anointed!
- I AM holy!
- I AM purified!
- I AM justified!
- I AM free-born!
- I AM saved and washed by the blood of the lamb!
- I AM born again!
- I AM a new creation!
- I AM free from guilt!
- I AM the light of the world!
- I AM God's delight!
- I AM beautiful/handsome!
- I AM created in God's image!
- I AM valuable!
- I AM victorious!
- I AM sovereign!
- I AM powerful!
- I AM the embodiment of the Creator, I AM!
- The great I AM dwells in me!
- I AM by grace!
- I renounce every vow, past, present, and future, that I made and is working against my divine purpose!
- I renounce every pledge, past, present, and future, working against my divine purpose!
- I renounce every oath I took, past, present, and future, that is sabotaging my divine purpose!
- I renounce every promise made, past, present, and future, affecting my life and destiny!
- I command my life to come in alignment with Christ's divine purpose, in Jesus' name!
- I call forth every negative word spoken in the past, present, and future, and I command them to scatter into oblivion!
- I declare that I do not exist in the past. I live right now!
- Heavenly Father, in the name of Jesus, I speak into my bloodline, genealogy, lineage, and ancestry today. I deny and refuse to bear any negative consequence that may hold me hostage in bondage!

- I renounce every oath, vow, pledge and promise that my ancestors made to the demonic entities in the sea, land, and heavens, stopping and opposing my divine purpose in life. I declare to them that I am free from their hold!
- I renounce every evil voice in my genealogy, bloodline, and genetics!
- I call forth all wicked records and contracts in my genealogy, past, present and future, and I declare my triumph over them!
- I call forth all the records in satanic archives in my ancestry past, present, and future. I decree that I am discharged and free!

Revoking Soul Contracts

Below are powerful words of prayer to sever all evil soul contract in your life.

In Jesus' name,

- I call forth the soul contracts between me and any individual or group of persons in the past, future and present binding, limiting and affecting my life. I, at this moment, revoke and cancel them in Jesus' name.
- I call forth any soul contract between me and any entity in the realm of the sea, land, second heaven, past, present, and future that's opposing my divine purpose. I revoke and cancel it in Jesus's name.
- I call forth every soul contract between me and any institution in the past, present, and future. I revoke them in Jesus's name.
- I call forth every soul contract from the databases of health, financial, or economic institutions, from my past, present, and future that serve as a barrier to my life. I revoke it right now.
- I call forth all the covenants and contracts in the past, present, or future from rituals and blood sacrifices working against me and my destiny. I revoke and cancel them.
- I call forth all the soul contracts with death in the past, present, and future, and I now revoke and cancel them.

- I call forth all the soul contracts in the database of wrong decision making, choices, partnerships, and relationships in my past, present, and future and hereby revoke and cancel them.
- I am a royal priest. I am a child of God; I do not exist in the past. I declare that I exist NOW. All the soul contracts with any person or group of persons, tribes, nationalities or genders that are holding me down, fueling accusations against me, limiting and binding me, I hereby revoke and cancel them.
- I call forth all the soul contracts formed against me by witches, wizards, sorcerers, false prophets, magicians, unfriendly friends, and envious witchcraft in the past, present and future affecting me negatively and opposing my divine purpose. I hereby render the contracts null and void in the name of Jesus.
- I revoke all agreements made consciously and unconsciously that gave another person or authority over me to limit or bind me or impose on me any evil load that is not mine in the mighty name of Jesus Christ.
- I call forth any soul contract made socially with cash, gifts, food, clothes, stationery items, books, and other tangible items in my past, present and future. I hereby revoke and cancel them in Jesus' mighty name.
- I call forth the soul contracts made with sororities and fraternities in my past, present and future. I cancel them and render them null and void.
- I call forth the soul contracts made electronically in my past, present, and future, rendering them null and void. I hereby revoke and cancel them in Jesus's name.
- I call forth the soul contracts (copies and backup copies) made with blood in my past, present, and future, and I render them null and void in the mighty name of Jesus Christ.
- I call forth the soul contracts from the record database in the spiritual realms on my destiny and revoke them in Jesus's name.
- I call forth the soul contracts from the record database in the spiritual realms on every reality in the past, present, and future, and I revoke them. The energies and gifts that I lost, I now reclaim them a hundredfold.

- I call forth the soul contracts from the record database in the spiritual realms on every dimension of my faith in the past, present and future and revoke them in Jesus's name.
- All the energies, time, and resources I have put into all these ungodly soul contracts, I reclaim them.
- I call forth all the backup copies of the contracts in all satanic databases in the world that are limiting my destiny, enflaming negative identities and accusations against me. I render those contracts null and void.
- I call forth all the contracts in the satanic archives and databases that have to do with murder, abortion, miscarriage, disability, loss of life, untimely deaths, divorce, and sudden deaths, and I render them null and void in the name of Jesus.
- I call forth all the contracts in satanic databases for bitterness, trauma, anger, rejection, failure, shame, poverty, lack, famine, and I revoke and cancel them in Jesus' name.
- I call forth all the contracts in my past, present, and future that are binding and limiting me, and I revoke them in the mighty name of Jesus Christ.
- I call forth the soul contracts from the record database in the spiritual realms on every level of my state of being in the past, present and future. I hereby revoke and cancel them in Jesus' mighty name.
- I call forth the soul contracts made with me socially in my past, present, and future, rendering them null and void.
- I come before Yahweh Elohim's throne and bring my petition to revoke all soul contracts opposing my divine purpose. Let the Lord send forth the angels of the Most High to sever all the soul ties as I refuse to continue to be oppressed and abused.
- Oh God, my Father, heal my wounded soul. I want to be made whole again. I want to fulfill my destiny. I claim my original divine self from the Father of lights. So shall it be. Let my life follow divine purposes from today forward. I am grateful. Thank you, Lord, AMEN.

Declarations

I seal these declarations and affirmations with the blood of Jesus, my shield, and my Savior.

I declare that these affirmations are binding.

I declare that these affirmations are not time-bound.

I declare my decision to alter my life experiences as declared above, beginning now and lasting forever. So shall it be in the mighty name of Jesus the Christ.

Author Information

Pastor J.E. Charles is the Founder and Senior Pastor of the Upper Room Fire Prayer Ministries and the Dunamis Christian Community Center, a non-denominational, Spirit-led, multi-cultural Christian organization in California, preaching the gospel of Jesus Christ.

His focus remains on passionate prayer to assist with deliverance and healing of people who are physically, emotionally, and spiritually sick. Some call him "a warrior to the core" when it comes to battling demonic and ungodly powers. His dedication to evangelizing, teaching, and preaching focus on a type of violent spiritual warfare. His motto states "The violent taketh it by force."

Pastor J. E. Charles came from a culture of overt battles with generational demonic forces that had established firm grasps of control over multiple connected people. He believes that open confrontation works best to take on the forces of darkness. He sees his mission as a way to teach and guide Christians to make bold, violent struggles against demonic threats. In turn, he will guide them to discover godly breakthroughs within themselves, their families, and communities.

'His leadership positions include Intercessory Prayer and Freedom Ministries at the Well Christian Community Church, a Minister with the Redeemed Christian Church of God (RCCG), and Mountain of Fire and Miracles Ministries in California. People who know him well bestowed upon the nickname, "Mr. Prayer."

Through these leadership roles, he offers insight into deliverance, wisdom as a prophet, godly ministry, and assists you to understand the revelations that affect your personal life. His goal is to align your life and spirit with God's word and power.

The glory of God's vision exists in Pastor J. E. Charles' heart, which allows him to serve the Dunamis Christian Community most fully. The deliverance and healing teams reach out and affect those who are trapped by ungodly forces and held captive by their sin. His ministry and that of the other leaders leads others to accept Christ, welcome Him into the hearts, and live in obedience to His direction.

Pastor J. E. Charles also delivers public speaking engagements, coaches people spiritually, has authored books and offers business management consultancy services.

Isaiah 5:13: "Therefore my people are gone into captivity, because they have no knowledge: and their honorable men are famished, and their multitude dried up with thirst."

Psalm 7:9: "Oh, let the wickedness of the wicked come to an end, but establish just."

Obadiah 1:17 "But upon Mount Zion shall be [deliverance], and there shall be holiness, and the house of Jacob shall possess their possession."

More books from J.E Charles

www.ingramcontent.com/pod-product-compliance
Lightning Source LLC
Chambersburg PA
CBHW050829160426
43192CB00010B/1949